# STRUCTURED PROGRAMMING
## A FIRST COURSE FOR STUDENTS AND HOBBYISTS

# STRUCTURED PROGRAMMING
## A FIRST COURSE FOR STUDENTS AND HOBBYISTS

PETER E. GOSLING

McGRAW-HILL Book Company (UK) Limited

**London** · New York · St Louis · San Francisco · Auckland
Bogotá · Guatemala · Hamburg · Johannesburg · Lisbon · Madrid
Mexico · Montreal · New Delhi · Panama · Paris · San Juan
São Paulo · Singapore · Sydney · Tokyo · Toronto

Published by
McGRAW-HILL Book Company (UK) Limited
MAIDENHEAD · BERKSHIRE · ENGLAND

---

British Library Cataloguing in Publication Data

Gosling, Peter E.
  Structured programming.
  1. Structured programming
  I. Title
  001.64'2        QA76.6

ISBN 0-07-084701-0


Library of Congress Cataloging in Publication Data

Gosling, P. E. (Peter E.)
  Structured programming.
  (Personal computer series)
  Includes index.
  1. Structured programming. I. Title. II. Series.
QA76.6.G675  1983        001.64'2        83-12013
ISBN 0-07-084701-0

12345 AP 86543

Printed and bound in Great Britain by The Alden Press, Oxford

# Contents

# Preface

This book is about programming but is in no way tied to any particular programming language. All the programs are written in a pseudo-code which may show some slight similarity to certain programming languages but in fact is a 'made-up' programming language. The reason for approaching the problem of writing a program in this way is to try to get through the barrier which many programming languages create between the user and the problem that is to be solved. It has been said that one of the greatest obstacles placed in a programmer's path is the GOTO statement. The excessive use of this word is the cause of too many 'spaghetti'-like programs which are difficult to follow and in many cases impossible to amend. All the pseudo-code programs in this book are written without a single GOTO in them. Instead the LOOP, REPEAT, and WHILE directives are used and these, together with the IF...THEN...ELSE construction, enable us to write programs which are far neater and tidier than those which are often written straight onto a keyboard. In the first half of the book the reader is introduced to a series of simple types of program written in our pseudo-code.These are then translated into the commoner types of BASIC in order to show how easy the final stage of producing code really is.

Unfortunately we are sometimes forced to use GOTO statements, even though some versions of BASIC now allow WHILE or REPEAT...UNTIL statements. You will see how we can convert pseudo-code loops into BASIC using as few of the GOTOs as possible.

The process of designing a program falls into several stages. The first of these is that of understanding the problem which is to be solved by the program. Second, we have to decide on an approach to the solution of that problem. Then we write down our solution, not nowadays in the form of a flowchart but in the form of a series of well-defined steps. These steps are usually stated in broad terms in the early stages of program development and are then continually refined until a completely logical program is obtained. This is often referred to as a 'top-down' approach where we are constantly going from the general to the particular. It also allows us to have a good look at the general form of the program before going into more detail. Finally, when a logically complete program has been obtained, the coding, into whatever language is required, can take place. The last operation represents about 5 per cent of the total programming effort. This approach should result in a program which is easier to code and stands a far better chance of working first time than one which has been produced by less formal methods. Research tends to confirm this observation.

Another advantage to writing programs in the structured way is that it is possible to make the production of working programs more of a communal effort. Groups of students in a class, for example, can work on separate parts of a project—one of the ten projects in the second half of the book for example. These can be brought together and finally coded when everyone is satisfied. Unsatisfactory modules can be rewritten without harming the others which form the rest of the project. This means that programs can be developed and written without the aid of a computer. Only at the very end of the work does the computer have to be brought in at all. This makes for a more realistic situation and a better understanding of what computing is all about. There was a time when the teaching of computer studies had to consist of teaching students to write programs in BASIC. Now things are changing and the teaching of computer studies in relation to the real world is far more important. By having a structured approach to programming, students can obtain a better idea of the way computers work and how they are used to solve real-life problems.

My sincere thanks to Peter Woollard for letting me use his BBC micro in the development of the programs written in BBC BASIC.

PETER GOSLING

# 1 INTRODUCTION

In the past few years there have been many books written about computer programming and almost without exception they have been 'How to write programs in BASIC', 'How to write programs in FORTRAN', and 'How to write programs in COBOL', or one of the many other computer languages. In fact, what usually happens is that these books have been written with very particular versions of the languages in mind. The result is that many of the programs listed in these texts will only run on certain makes of computer and in one special version of the language.

BASIC, being the most popular computer language for the rapidly growing microcomputer market, is the language which suffers most from a lack of standardization and a program in BASIC which runs on an Apple II will often not run on a BBC Model B, a Commodore 8032, or any other micro, without major surgery being performed on it. It is not that the **program** is incorrect but that the **coding** of that program into BASIC is not compatible with that 'spoken' by the microcomputer being used. It is important to construct logical sequences of events which will result in a certain problem being solved. When that sequence, which we call a **program**, is complete then it can be coded into whatever version of BASIC, or any other language for that matter, is required to be run on the computer. In other words, programming is about **logic**, not about a programming language. We only use the languages which have become available because they are each very good for implementing certain kinds of program. For example, FORTRAN is very useful if we have to perform a lot of mathematical and logical operations since it is a FORmula TRANslator. Every language has its own strengths and weaknesses. It is probably true to say that if you are going to solve a problem using a computer the designing of the solution takes about 95 per cent of the time and the coding into a language, say BASIC, takes about 5 per cent of the time and comes when all the other work has been done. Being a programmer can often be a rather boring and repetitive

1

job if all you have to do is to code other people's program specifications into a computer language. The really interesting and creative part comes from the program design. That is why this book is about writing programs—but not writing programs with a specific version of BASIC in mind. BASIC is only used because it is such a common and popular language, and we will see how easy it is to convert from the logical program into several versions of BASIC. In fact, it would be quite simple to convert any of the programs in this book into one of a number of languages: Pascal, FORTRAN, or any one of the many BASICs now available.

Many people new to programming find there is a great temptation to sit down at a keyboard and write a program then and there. This might be all right for a very simple calculation-type program but is very dangerous if one is intending to write a program of any consequence. This is where good program design comes in and the techniques demonstrated later will hopefully be of value. Until recently the flowchart was the vehicle for designing programs, but flowcharts are notoriously tortuous to follow and very hard work to amend. By using the structured approach featured in the examples which follow, together with what is called a 'top-down' approach, we can write programs which are easier to follow, much easier to amend, and work more efficiently.

There is another point which emerges from this change of approach to programming. It is that there is a very serious problem arising, in schools in particular, where there is likely to be no more than one microcomputer per class of perhaps 30. If programming is to be taught, then it can be made into a group activity, especially when the problem being solved can be broken down into a series of separate parts. Groups of pupils, or even single pupils, can be given separate and specific parts of the program to write and these can be tested individually. When all the separate parts are certified to be satisfactory, then the coding into BASIC can begin. By doing this the discipline of programming is easier to acquire and the results become far more satisfying. It then becomes easier to write more useful and meaningful programs. The end result is also achieved in the manner in which it is carried out in real life, where programmers tend to work in teams.

Good techniques of documentation of programs are a useful spin-off from this sort of activity. In fact the documentation of programs is worthy of a complete book all on its own, and so is not being covered in anything but a very simple way here.

So what is this 'top-down' and structured approach to writing programs? Essentially the technique is to provide a logical sequence of events when solving a problem, and because we use computers to solve problems we have to write computer programs to help us do this. First of all we have to understand the problem we are about to solve. This is not as silly as it sounds since there is no point in solving a problem if we are unsure of exactly what the problem is in the first place and what the implications of the problem are. Second, we have to devise some method of obtaining a solution to our problem. For example, we may know that there is a formula that we can use or a particular technique that will give us the answer. These methods are pencil and paper methods that we want to translate into instructions the computer can carry out. The computer will only solve problems in the same way as we can, but far quicker and more accurately. Very often we are able to ask a computer to employ methods we would not dream of using ourselves simply because of the time they would take and the boring repetition of the method. Luckily computers never get bored and take happily to repetitive tasks. We can only devise our solution by writing it down. This is where the top-down approach comes in. Once we have understood what the solution to the problem requires we can start to write down in general terms how we are to solve it. All that is required is to write down a sequence of events in much the same way as we used to draw an outline flowchart of the type shown in Figure 1.1 (page 5). Here the problem to be solved is that of deciding which steps to take if we are to search through a list of names in order to find out if a particular name exists on the list. People who look at a flowchart such as this for the first time are often thrown off balance because it expresses in a two dimensional form a sequence which is in essence only one dimensional. The fact that one can only take one path at a time around the chart is not always easy to see, particularly because there are two 'stop' points in this chart. Surely the method of searching is easier to understand if we write down our steps in the following manner, which is an attempt at a 'top-down' approach to the solution to the problem:

1. Read the name being searched for into memory.
2. Extract the first name from the list held in memory.
3. If the name read in and the name from the list match then print "Name found" and stop.

4. Otherwise if there are any more names on the list extract the next name from the list and go back to step 3.
5. If there are no more names on the list print "Name not found".
6. Stop.

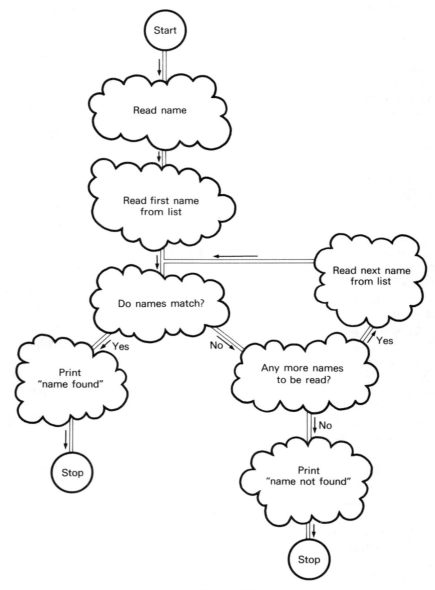

**Figure 1.1.**

Already this solution is falling into the 'GOTO' trap. This is the trap which leads to many programs looking like a heap of spaghetti with paths off to all parts of themselves and becoming almost impossible to understand as a result. There are certain very eminent computer professionals who expressly forbid the use of GOTO statements in programs and it must be said that their continued use is often an obstacle to simple programming. Sometimes a particular version of BASIC forces the use of GOTO, but every effort is made in this book to reduce its use. There are several other statements which are far more meaningful than the GOTO and these will be used whenever possible. In the programs in this book we shall use the words LOOP, REPEAT, WHILE, and UNTIL together with IF, THEN, and ELSE to complete our top down approach to our first problem. This becomes:

1. Read the name being searched for into memory.
2. Read the first name from the list into memory.
3. Loop until there are no more names left to be read.
4. If the name being searched for matches the name from the list.
5. Then print "Name found". Stop.
6. Else read the next name from the list into memory.
7. Repeat.
8. Print "Name not found".
9. Stop.

The structure of the program then can be made more apparent by writing it rather more formally as:

1. Read the name being searched for into memory.
2. Read the first name from the list into memory.
3. Loop until there are no more names left to be read.
4.    If the name being searched for matches the name from the list
5.       Then
6.          Print "Name found".
7.          Stop.
8.       Else
9.          Read the next name from the list into memory.
10.   Ifend.
11. Repeat.
12. Print "Name not found".
13. Stop.

Note the improvement in clarity by the use of indenting. The lines 3 and 11 enclose the main loop of the program and lines 5 to 7 show what happens if a match is found and whatever follows the 'else' in line 8 is what happens when a match is not found. In fact, what has been done is to write the instructions in a slightly more formal way than just : 'Read the name to be searched for and then read through the names in the list, testing them in turn against the name. When you find a match say so and stop searching. If you get to the end of the list without finding a match then issue a message to that effect.'

All the problems which follow are solved in this way. The top-down approach can be refined into more detail and leads us to a formal representation of the solution written in what is called a 'pseudo-code'. This is a formal translation of the above program into something more like a computer program where names are used for memory locations. These will be shown in heavy type, such as **list** or **number**, and so on. The final move from pseudo-code to computer program is then quite simple if we draw up a data table which lists all the variable names used in our pseudo-code, what they are representing, and the BASIC variable names used in the final program.

As you go through the book you will notice that the symbol :=
is used as well as the = sign. This is because in most programming languages the = sign performs two functions. One of these is the **assignment** function and the other is as a statement of equality, the two being quite different from each other. In a BASIC statement such as

$$A = A + B$$

we mean that the value to be **assigned** to the variable called A is obtained by adding the current value of the variable A to the current value of the variable B. Hence whatever was stored in A is replaced by a new value. What we are doing is to perform the operations of copying the numbers stored in particular memory locations into the part of the computer which performs arithmetic, adding them together, and placing the answer in a named location. In no way are we saying that somehow something called A is made equal to the sum of something called A and something called B. In this book we shall use the := together with the word 'LET' in order to make the distinction between the 'assignment' situation and the 'equality' situation.

The use of the = sign in computer languages concerns the equality of two numbers by saying 'IF the value of the number stored in A is equal to the number stored in B THEN something has to happen'. If the equality does not exist then some alternative has to happen; hence the use of

IF (some assertion is true) THEN (do something) ELSE (do something else)
Occasionally the 'something else' does not exist, in which case we say 'do nothing' or SKIP. The 'somethings' we do may be more than one operation, in which case we can list them—but indented in order to improve clarity. For example:

IF bank account is greater than price of suit
   THEN
      Visit bank
      Draw out money
      Buy new suit
   ELSE
      Do nothing
IFEND

Notice how we bracket the IF with an IFEND so that we know where the conditicnal operations begin and end.
    We can test other things as well as equality. We can test, in fact, for six relationships existing between a pair of numbers. The six are:

| | Relationship | Symbol |
|---|---|---|
| 1. | Equal to | = |
| 2. | Greater than | > |
| 3. | Less than | < |
| 4. | Greater than or equal to | >= |
| 5. | Less than or equal to | <= |
| 6. | Not equal to | <> |

    As we proceed through this text we shall see that we can test for the above relationships between any pair of variables, or strings of characters, stored in the computer's memory so that we can test to see whether one number is greater than another or if the set of characters making up the name 'Fred' comes before (is less than) the set of characters making up the name 'Bill'.

# 2 GETTING STARTED

Designing and writing a program simply to perform calculations is very easy. Once we know what numbers have to be input into the computer's memory, so that they can be manipulated in a formula, our task becomes very simple. For example, suppose we needed to compute the simple interest earned by a sum of money, the Principal, for a certain number of years, the Time, at a particular Rate per cent, then the formula

$$I=(PxTxR)/100$$

is all that is required. So if we write:

```
1. READ principal, time, rate
2. LET interest:=(principal*time*rate)/100
3. PRINT interest
4. END
```

we have produced a program. All that is needed now is to transform this set of logical steps into a computer language understood by our particular computer. Before this step is taken we should produce a data table. This lists all the variables by name as used in the logical program and in our final BASIC program:

| Logical name | Purpose | Type | BASIC variable name |
|---|---|---|---|
| **principal** | amount of money invested | real | PRINCIPAL |
| **time** | number of years of investment | real | TIME |
| **rate** | rate per cent | real | RATE |
| **interest** | amount of interest earned | real | INTEREST |

We can divide the variables we use into various types. Each has its own special way of being stored inside the computer's memory. Some versions of languages take account of these, others do not. The main types are **real** numbers which take up four bytes of storage, **integer** numbers which take up two bytes of storage, and **string** variables where each character in the string takes up one byte of storage. In addition we can have **double precision** numbers if we need very great accuracy. All these variables can be held in **arrays**, lists, or tables in memory. The distinction between the various types of variables in the different BASICs is indicated by the use of $,%, and # after the variable name. By organizing the storage of the data used in the program we can make both the efficiency of the program as high as possible and the amount of memory used by the program as low as possible:

```
10 INPUT PRINCIPAL,TIME,RATE
20 INTEREST=(PRINCIPAL*TIME*RATE)/100
30 PRINT INTEREST
```

If we should wish to amend the program, to calculate the amount obtained by adding the principal to the interest, for example, then it is very easy to amend one line and add another:

```
1. READ principal, time, rate
2. LET interest:=(principal*time*rate)/100
3. LET amount:=interest+principal
4. PRINT interest,amount
5. END
```

Our data table would become:

| Logical name | Purpose | Type | BASIC variable name |
|---|---|---|---|
| **principal** | amount of money invested | real | PRINCIPAL |
| **time** | number. of years of investment | real | TIME |
| **rate** | rate per cent | real | RATE |

**10**

| interest | amount of interest earned | real | INTEREST |
|---|---|---|---|
| amount | total value of investment | real | AMOUNT |

and our BASIC program would be:

```
10 INPUT PRINCIPAL,TIME,RATE
20 INTEREST=(PRINCIPAL*TIME*RATE)/100
30 AMOUNT=INTEREST+PRINCIPAL
40 PRINT INTEREST,AMOUNT
```

Problems which simply perform calculations are very easy to write once one becomes used to the special features of the version of BASIC in use at the time. It is the facility offered by all programming languages for the control of repetitive calculations that starts to use a computer for real work. Computers are far more than just sophisticated calculating machines.

Loops tend to fall into three categories. The first of these says, 'Do the following operations until a particular situation occurs.' The second says, 'Repeat all the following while this condition holds.' The third type of loop says, 'Perform the following for a certain set of values of some control variable.'

All these loops must have a start and a finish clearly marked. For example, a loop of the first kind might be:

1. Loop.
2. Read a number.
3. Add the number into a total.
4. Repeat until the total exceeds 50.
5. Print the total.

In pseudo-code we could write:

```
1. LET total:=0
2. LOOP
3.    READ number
4.    LET total:=total+number
5. REPEAT UNTIL total>50
6. PRINT total
```

Note the indentation within the loop. This gives added clarity. A data table will be:

| Logical name | Purpose | Type | BASIC variable name |
|---|---|---|---|
| **number** | any number | real | NUMBER |
| **total** | total | real | TOTAL |

A program in 'standard' BASIC might be:

```
10 TOTAL=0
20 INPUT NUMBER
30 TOTAL=TOTAL+NUMBER
40 IF TOTAL<=50 THEN GOTO 20
60 PRINT TOTAL
```

Notice how this program has only one GOTO instruction. If one sat down to write the program without thinking about it first there is a strong chance that it would have several of these. However, if we use the version of the language offered on the BBC computer we can write:

```
10 SUM = 0
20 REPEAT
30    INPUT NUMBER
40    SUM = SUM + NUMBER
50 UNTIL SUM>50
60 PRINT SUM
```

NOTE: BBC BASIC does not like variable names which start with the same letters as any of their "reserved" words.

A LOOP WHILE loop can cover the same situation if we write:

```
1. LET total:=0
2. LOOP WHILE total<=50
3.    READ number
4.    LET total:=total+number
5. REPEAT
6. PRINT total
```

and using a version of BASIC which allows WHILE to be used, not all of them unfortunately, we get:

```
10 TOTAL=0
20 WHILE TOTAL<=50
30    INPUT NUMBER
40    TOTAL=TOTAL+NUMBER
50 WEND
60 PRINT TOTAL
```

Whereas in the more usual form of BASIC we would have to write

```
10 TOTAL=0
20 IF TOTAL>50 THEN GOTO 60
30 INPUT NUMBER
40 TOTAL=TOTAL+NUMBER
50 GOTO 20
60 PRINT TOTAL
```

If a REPEAT...UNTIL loop is used then the program will always go through that loop at least once. On the other hand, a REPEAT WHILE...loop might never be executed if the value of the variable controlling the repetition does not fulfil the condition at the start of the loop.

The first lines of these programs all set the variable TOTAL to zero. This is called **initializing**. Most BASICs tend to set all variables to zero without being asked before the program is executed, but it is good practice to set counting variables and totalling variables to some initial value, often zero, before getting into the program. Notice the tests which have to be made in the IF statements. These tend to be the opposite of the tests by the WHILE and the REPEAT conditions.

When placing a set of numbers into memory it is common practice to have a 'rogue' value, often zero, at the end of the list to signify that there are no more numbers coming. Our program has to be always on the lookout for this number and so we write:

```
1. LET total:=0
2. READ number
3. LOOP
4.    LET total:=total+number
5.    READ number
6. REPEAT UNTIL number=0
7. PRINT total
```

or

```
1. LET total:=0
2. READ number
3. LOOP WHILE number<>0
4.    LET total:=total+number
5.    READ number
6. REPEAT
7. PRINT number
```

## which can be written as:

```
10 SUM=0                              10 TOTAL=0
20 INPUT NUMBER                       20 INPUT NUMBER
30 REPEAT                             30 WHILE NUMBER<>0
40    SUM=SUM+NUMBER       or         40    TOTAL=TOTAL+NUMBER
50    INPUT NUMBER                    50    INPUT NUMBER
60 UNTIL NUMBER = 0                   60 WEND
70 PRINT SUM                          70 PRINT TOTAL
```

## whereas using IF and GOTO we have to write:

```
10 TOTAL=0                            10 TOTAL=0
20 INPUT NUMBER          or           20 INPUT NUMBER
30 TOTAL=TOTAL+NUMBER                 30 IF NUMBER=0 THEN GOTO 60
40 IF NUMBER<>0 THEN GOTO 20          40 TOTAL=TOTAL + NUMBER
50 PRINT TOTAL                        50 GOTO 20
                                      60 PRINT TOTAL
```

The last two programs are more difficult to write because the writer has to remember the line numbers where special operations take place, especially if they are on lines whose numbers do not yet exist—at line 30 in the last example. Hence the use of REPEAT or WHILE statements if they are available. They also make the program (1) easier to understand and (2) easier to amend, as we shall see later on.

Finally we have the IF...THEN...ELSE type of statement. This enables us to make decisions and go on one of two distinct paths depending on the outcome of the decision. To take a simple example let us look at a program which decides whether a number is odd or even. To start with we can write:

1. Read a number.
2. If it is odd then print "ODD"; if not then print "EVEN".
3. End.

Next we have to decide exactly how our computer will know if the number is odd or even; contrary to popular opinion they are not magic! We can do this by dividing the number by two and seeing if we get a remainder:

1. Read a number.
2. Divide the number by two.
3. If there is a remainder print "ODD".
4. Otherwise print "EVEN".
5. End.

So how do we tell if there is a remainder? Well, all except the very tiny versions of BASIC have built-in functions so that we can evaluate sines, square roots, logarithms as well as the whole number, or integer, part of a number. It does this by chopping off everything which follows the decimal point. Let us, for the time being, call this function CHOP:

1. Read a number.
2. Divide the number by two.
3. If CHOP(result)<>result then print "ODD".
4. Otherwise print "EVEN".
5. End.

The decision in line 3 says that if the number is changed by having its decimal part removed then it must be an odd number. If it is unchanged then it must be an even number. For example, if the number was 13 then the result of division by two gives us 6.5. Taking away the decimal part leaves us with 6. As 6.5 and 6 are not the same, the original number was an odd number. Now let us write this in pseudo-code:

```
1. READ number
2. LET result:=number/2
3. IF CHOP(result)<>result
4.    THEN
5.       PRINT "ODD"
6.    ELSE
7.       PRINT "EVEN"
8. IFEND
```

Here is our data table:

| Logical name | Purpose | Type | BASIC variable name |
|---|---|---|---|
| **number** | any number | real | NUMBER |
| **result** | result of division of **number** by 2 | real | RESULT |

and our BASIC program becomes:

```
10 INPUT NUMBER
20 RESULT=NUMBER/2
30 IF INT(RESULT)<>RESULT THEN PRINT "ODD" ELSE PRINT "EVEN"
```

The BASIC function INT does the job of our CHOP.

# 3 EXAMPLES

## Example 1—Loops

In this problem we are going to write a program which will add up a series of numbers and print their total and the average of the numbers for us.

First of all we have to consider just what we would have to do if we were going to do the problem using a pencil, paper, and a calculator. Obviously we will have to accumulate the running total of the numbers and also we need to know how many numbers there are. We need this information if we are going to calculate the average; average = total/how many. Remember that we will start off with a clean sheet of paper and this means that at that point we will have no running total, having not yet processed any of the numbers. So at the start of operations we have to set both the running total and the count of how many numbers we have processed so far to zero. Then we examine the numbers one at a time and as we deal with each one we add it into the running total and remind ourselves that one more number has been processed. Then we process the next number, and so on. But how do we know when to stop the calculation part, which is a 'loop', and go into the final phase of calculating the average and printing it together with the total of all the numbers? We can see with our eyes when the last number of a list has been reached, but how do we tell the computer that ? There are in fact several ways and the one we are going to use here is that of putting a 'rogue' number at the end of the list. This rogue value can be any number, but we often use a zero or $-1$, and we tell the computer to always be on the lookout for that number as that is our way of telling the machine that it has had all the information it is going to get for the time being. On detecting this rogue value the computer can jump out of its loop and will then proceed to do the calculation of the average and the necessary printing. Our solution can now be written down as:

1. Initialize **count** and **total**.
2. Read numbers in one at a time, terminating with a zero.

3. Add each number into the **total**.
4. Increase the **count** by one.
5. When a zero is input divide the **total** by the **count** giving the **average**.
6. Print the **total** and the **average**.

So far, so good, but it is not formal enough at this stage as we need to specify not only what variable names we are going to use but also the kind of tests and loops we are going to have. Our program then refines to become:

```
1. LET total:=0
2. LET count:=0
3. LOOP
4.    READ number
5.    LET total:=total+number
6.    LET count:=count+1
7. REPEAT UNTIL number=0
8. LET average:=total/(count-1)
9. PRINT total,average
10.END
```

Next we should draw up our data table. Remember that this specifies the names of the variables we have used in our logical construction and the names we are going to use for them in our particular programming language.

| Logical name | Purpose | Type | BASIC variable name |
|---|---|---|---|
| **total** | running total | real | TOTAL |
| **count** | counter for number of numbers processed | integer | COUNT% |
| **average** | average | real | AVERAGE |
| **number** | number in list | real | NUMBER |

We make the BASIC variable COUNT an integer—hence the % sign after the name—because we want to make sure that the counter increases by one and only one and not by the .999999999 or 1.000000001 that computers tend to use instead of unity.

In BASIC the program becomes:

```
10 TOTAL = 0:COUNT%=0
20 INPUT NUMBER
30 TOTAL = TOTAL + NUMBER
40 COUNT% = COUNT% + 1
50 IF NUMBER = 0 THEN GOTO 70
60 GOTO 20
70 AVERAGE=TOTAL/(COUNT%-1)
80 PRINT TOTAL, AVERAGE
90 END
```

Notice that we have used the BASIC word INPUT rather than READ in our program. This is because it is easy to test the program out at this stage by just typing 'RUN' and typing in the numbers one at a time. This will cause the program to execute in 'slow motion' so that we can check that it really does work. Then we can change any parts of it to suit different circumstances, as indeed we shall do later on in the book.

There is another way we could write the program in BASIC provided our version of the language has the ability to accept REPEAT statements, as with the BBC version of BASIC. In this case the program becomes:

```
10 SUM = 0:INDEX%=0
20 REPEAT
30   INPUT NUMBER
40   SUM=SUM + NUMBER
50   INDEX%=INDEX%+1
60 UNTIL NUMBER=0
70 AVERAGE=SUM/(INDEX% - 1)
80 PRINT SUM,AVERAGE
90 END
```

This particular program illustrates an important feature of REPEAT UNTIL loops. It is that the testing for the condition which completes the loop is made at the end of the loop. In this case on line 30 NUMBER is input, then added to SUM, and then INDEX% is increased by one. But if NUMBER had been zero, as it is when it closes the loop, then zero is added to SUM, INDEX% becomes one greater, and hence we have to divide SUM by one less than we would have done if we had made the test for the value of NUMBER at the start of the loop, as we do with a WHILE statement.

A better use of REPEAT UNTIL would be to write:

```
10 SUM = 0:INDEX%=0
20 INPUT NUMBER
30 REPEAT
40   SUM=SUM + NUMBER
50   INDEX%=INDEX%+1
60   INPUT NUMBER
70 UNTIL NUMBER=0
80 AVERAGE=SUM/INDEX%
90 PRINT SUM,AVERAGE
100END
```

If we use WHILE we would write:

```
1.  LET total:=0
2.  LET count:=0
3.  READ number
4.  LOOP WHILE number<>0
5.    LET total:=total+number
6.    LET count:=count+1
7.    READ number
8.  REPEAT
9.  LET average:=total/count
10. PRINT total,average
11. END
```

## In 'ordinary' BASIC this becomes:

```
10 TOTAL=0:COUNT%=0
20 INPUT NUMBER
30 IF NUMBER=0 THEN GOTO 70
40 TOTAL = TOTAL + NUMBER
50 COUNT%=COUNT%+1
60 GOTO 20
70 AVERAGE=TOTAL/COUNT%
80 PRINT TOTAL,AVERAGE
90 END
```

## Using a BASIC with the WHILE facility it becomes:

```
10 TOTAL=0:COUNT%=0
20 INPUT NUMBER
30 WHILE NUMBER<>0
40   TOTAL = TOTAL + NUMBER
50   COUNT%=COUNT%+1
60   INPUT NUMBER
70 WEND
80 AVERAGE=TOTAL/COUNT%
90 PRINT TOTAL,AVERAGE
100END
```

You should notice that in both cases the loop has to be 'seeded' with a value for the variable called NUMBER. This is because the loop has got to know about the size of the number held in the variable; if a WHILE loop is used then the loop will not be traversed at all if NUMBER is zero, and most versions of BASIC will set all variables to zero as soon as 'RUN' is keyed in. If the REPEAT...UNTIL loop is traversed it has to be executed at least once because the test lies at the end of the loop. These are examples of 'preconditioned' and 'postconditioned' loops. A preconditioned loop is only executed if the condition holds. A postconditioned loop is executed and then the test is made.

## Example 2—Handling strings

This next example uses the concept of a string of characters. Our problem is that of counting the number of vowels which occur in a word and printing out what that number is. We therefore need initially to assemble our thoughts in the following manner:

1. Initialize variables.
2. Read in a word.
3. Take each letter of the word in turn and test it against a vowel.
4. If a match is found with any one of the vowels–increase the vowel count by one.
5. Print the vowel count.

At least this gives us a starting point, but we have to remember that we have to tell the computer just what a vowel is; it has no means of knowing unless we tell it. So we have to set up a list of acceptable letters—"AEIOU"—against which every letter in our word is tested. If a match with any one of these is found then our vowel count is increased by one. So now we can write:

1. Set the vowel count to zero.
2. Set up a string of vowels, "AEIOU".
3. Read in the word.
4. Test every letter in our word against each of the vowels in turn.
5. If a match is found increase the vowel count by one.
6. If the vowel count is zero then print "No vowels found"; else print the vowel count.
7. End.

Step 4 of our program is quite complex and involves two loops, one inside the other. First, we have to select each letter in turn from our word and then test this letter against each letter of the set of vowels in turn. This means that we have to perform up to five tests, there being five vowels to choose from, on each of the letters in our word. Step 4 can then be expanded to be:

4a. Loop for the number of letters in the word, starting at the first letter.
4b. Loop for the five letters in the vowel list starting at the first vowel.
4c. Test the letter from the word against the letter from the vowel list.
4d. If there is a match
4e. Then.
4f. increase vowel count by one.

4g.　　　Else
4h.　　　　Do nothing.
4i.　　Ifend.
4j.　　Repeat
4k. Repeat.

Now let us rewrite the above in pseudo-code:

```
1.  LET vowel:=0
2.  LET vowel$:="AEIOU"
3.  READ word$
4.  LOOP FOR i=1 TO lengthword
5.    LOOP FOR j=1 to 5
6.      IF word$(i)=vowel$(j)
7.        THEN
8             LET vowel:=vowel+1
9.        ELSE
10.            SKIP
11.    IFEND
12.   REPEAT
13. REPEAT
14. IF vowel=0
15.   THEN
16.     PRINT "No vowels in the word"
17.   ELSE
18.     PRINT vowel;"vowels"
19. IFEND
20. END
```

Notice how we use **vowel** for the vowel count and **vowel\$** to represent the string which contains the vowel list; hence **vowel\$**(3) would stand for the third vowel in the list which is 'I'.

Our data table will be:

| Logical name | Purpose | Type | BASIC variable name |
|---|---|---|---|
| **vowel** | vowel count | real | VOWEL |
| **vowel\$** | string of vowels | string | VOWEL\$ |
| **word\$** | word to be tested | string | WORD\$ |
| **lengthword** | number. of letters in **word\$** | integer | LENGTH% |
| **i** | index to letter in **word\$** | integer | I% |

| | | | |
|---|---|---|---|
| j | index to vowel in **vowel$** | integer | J% |

Now let us write a program in BASIC so that we can test our ideas:

```
10 VOWEL = 0
20 VOWEL$="AEIOU"
30 INPUT WORD$
40 LENGTH%=LEN(WORD$)
50 FOR I%=1 TO LENGTH%
60 FOR J%=1 TO 5
70 IF MID$(WORD$,I%,1)=MID$(VOWEL$,J%,1) THEN VOWEL=VOWEL+1
80 NEXT J%
90 NEXT I%
100 IF VOWEL=0 THEN PRINT "NO VOWELS IN THE WORD"ELSE PRINT VOWEL;"VOWELS"
110 END
```

Having got to the stage where our program works the next stage is to see if we can improve it. Note that the BASIC program can be written in a number of ways depending on the version of BASIC available and our skill at using it, but we can use this program as the basis of many more. A good way to solve a problem is to solve a simpler problem first; when that is solved we can use our solution as a basis of a solution to a more complicated problem. Our simplified problem can lead us on to writing a program which will not just find how many vowels there are in a word but how many of each particular vowel was present. Another point we could well consider is that before we begin analysing a word for vowels we should really make sure that we are analysing a set of characters which are worth analysing. In other words, we should make sure that we are not wasting valuable computer time trying to process rubbish. So before we even start testing for vowels we should validate the data—**word$**—to see that it only contains the letters of the alphabet and not characters such as %,&,8, or ;. Project 10 in fact develops this idea considerably.

## Example 3—Lists

In this example we are going to start off by scanning a list of numbers in order to find which number in the list is the largest. This is an easy job for humans to perform but not so easy for a computer which has no experience of 'large' or 'small' to draw on. We can cast our eye over the list and the largest is easily noticeable. Our program will make the computer scan the list and do a similar thing, but because we are dealing with a machine we have to tell it how it is to pick out the largest number in the list.

First of all we have to present the list to the computer and get it to store this in its memory. Then we tell it to look along the list and find the largest and finally print it out. Our first attempt at a design for this program would look like this:

1. Read the list into memory.
2. Scan the list from start to finish and pick out the largest number in the list.
3. Print the largest number.

That looks very simple but it begs a very large number of questions. The first of these is the placing of the list in memory. Just how will we do this and manage to distinguish between the different numbers in the list? We can do this if we call the various members of the list by a general name followed by an 'index' telling us their positions in the list. We use this idea when we number houses in a street and call them 'No.1 Park Road', 'No.2 Park Road', and so on to the end of the street. We can call the numbers in the list 'List(1)', 'List(2)', etc. The number in brackets is the index to the items in the list so that the seventh number in the list is called 'List(7)'. So to read the numbers into memory our first step becomes:

1. Loop for the number of numbers in the list.
2.     Read **list(index)**.
3.     Increase **index** by 1.
4. Repeat.

At first sight that seems fine except that although we have said that **index** is to be increased by one as we go through the loop there is no way of knowing what its initial value is to be. We know that we should start counting at one, but the computer, being the kind of machine it is, will probably start counting at zero unless we tell it otherwise. So we must have:

1. Initialize **index** to 1.
2. Loop for the number of numbers in the list.
3.     Read **list(index)**.
4.     Increase **index** by 1.
5. Repeat.

But how does the computer know when the end of the list has been reached ? When there is nothing else to read ? We cannot do this because if we tell a computer to read a number and there is no number to read it tends to imagine that there is an error, stops, and tells us so. Computers are very bad at dealing with the unexpected unless we set a trap to catch the error before the computer does. We can prepare for this kind of error by saying that the last number it is going to be presented with is a 'rogue' value again. This will cause it to stop the reading part of the program and start the next part. In our case we are going to use the number zero to act as our rogue and so we have to get our program to be on the lookout for this number right from the very start. So now we write:

1. Initialize **index** to 1.
2. Loop while **list(index)**<>0.
3.    Read **list(index)**.
4.    Increase **index** by 1.
5. Repeat.

Finally, before moving on to the next part of our program we have to do one more thing. We have to make a declaration that we are going to use an 'array' which is called by the name **list** and that it is going to contain a maximum of 100 numbers. This is necessary because computers have to arrange their storage in as effective a way as possible and so we have to make a declaration which is rather like reserving rooms in an hotel. In order to make the best use of the computer's memory we like to have all the elements of a list next door to each other if possible and so we reserve this space by stating:

1. Reserve up to 100 memory locations for the numbers forming the array called **list**.
2. Initialize **index** to 1.
3. Loop while **list(index)**<>0.
4.    Read **list(index)**.
5.    Increase **index** by 1.
6. Repeat.

In pseudo-code this becomes:

```
1. ARRAY list(1:100)      Note how we have read
2. LET index:=1           the first item into
3. READ list(index)       the list before entering
                          the loop.
```

24

```
4.  LOOP WHILE list(index)<>0
5.    LET index:=index+1
6.      READ list(index)
7.  REPEAT
8.  LET length:=index-1
```

Now we can get on with the main part of the problem which is to find which number in the list, which is now stored safely in memory, is the largest. To do this we have to realize that our computer can only do one thing at a time, even though what it does is performed at incredible speed. This means that it can make mistakes at an incredible speed as well! So we imagine our computer scanning through the list and dealing with one number at a time. Because it cannot look ahead we have to realize that the first number it sees in the list is undoubtedly the largest so far. This means that we can write:

8. Set **largest** to be the value of **list**(1).

Then we can get on and compare all the other members of the list with the current largest. If any member in the list exceeds the size of the current largest then its value is taken by the largest. If not, we go on to the next in the list. By now all the list is in memory and we know just how many items the list contains because the length of the list has been preserved in the variable called **length**. But note that the number of numbers in the list is one less than the number of numbers we read in—the last number was a 'rogue' value not to be counted. Thus we write:

9. Loop for the length of the list starting with an **index** of 2.
10.If **list(index)>largest**
11.    Then
12.        Replace **largest** with **list(index)**.
13.    Else
14.        Do nothing.
15.Ifend.
16.Repeat.

Finally, having reached the end of the list we merely print the value of the variable called **largest**.

17.Print **largest**

So now we can write the whole program in pseudo-code. We have already done the first seven lines so we will add the new parts onto the end of those:

```
1.  ARRAY list(1:100)
2.  LET index:=1
3.  READ list(index)
4.  LOOP WHILE list(index)<>0
5.    LET index:=index+1
6.    READ list(index)
7.  REPEAT
8.  LET length:=index-1
9.  LET largest:=list(1)
10 LOOP for index=2 to length
11.   IF list(index)>largest
12.     THEN
13.       LET largest:=list(index)
14.     ELSE
15.       SKIP
16.   IFEND
17.REPEAT
18.PRINT largest
19.END
```

We will now translate our logical program into one of the dialects of BASIC in order to run it. Our data table will be:

| Logical name | Purpose | Type | BASIC variable name |
|---|---|---|---|
| **list** | list of numbers | numeric array index (1:100) | L |
| **index** | index to **list** | integer | INDEX% |
| **length** | length of **list** | integer | LENGTH% |
| **largest** | largest number | real | LARGEST |

and the BASIC program will be:

```
10 DIM L(100)
20 INDEX%=1
30 INPUT L(INDEX%)
40 IF L(INDEX%)=0 THEN GOTO 70
50 INDEX%=INDEX%+1
60 GOTO 30
70 LENGTH%=INDEX%-1
80 LARGEST=L(1)
90 FOR INDEX%=2 TO LENGTH%
100 IF L(INDEX%)>LARGEST THEN LARGEST=L(INDEX%)
110 NEXT INDEX%
120 PRINT LARGEST
130 END
```

The above is a program using the standard, if such a thing really exists, version of the BASIC language. Here is another version using WHILE and WEND for the input loop. Notice that we have written another BASIC program without GOTO statements:

```
10 DIM L(100)
20 INDEX%=1
30 INPUT L(INDEX%)
40 WHILE L(INDEX%)<>0
50    INDEX%=INDEX%+1
60    INPUT L(INDEX%)
70 WEND
80 LENGTH%=INDEX%-1
90 LARGEST=L(1)
100 FOR INDEX%=2 TO LENGTH%
110 IF L(INDEX%)>LARGEST THEN LARGEST=L(INDEX%)
120 NEXT INDEX%
130 PRINT LARGEST
140 END
```

Having solved this problem we are now in a position to solve another problem which is very similar. This is the problem of finding the smallest number in a list. For this we have only to alter four lines in our logical program. These are lines 9,11,13, and 18,which must become:

```
9. LET smallest:= list(1)
11.IF list(index)<smallest
13.LET smallest:=list(index)
18.PRINT smallest
```

and so we get:

```
1. ARRAY list(1:100)
2. LET index:=1
3. READ list(index)
4. LOOP WHILE list(index)<>0
5.    LET index:=index+1
6.    READ list(index)
7. REPEAT
8. LET length:=index-1
9. LET smallest:=list(1)
10.LOOP for index=2 to length
11.   IF list(index)<smallest
12.      THEN
13.         LET smallest:=list(index)
14.      ELSE
15.         SKIP
16.   IFEND
17.REPEAT
18.PRINT smallest
19.END
```

It now becomes very simple to make the program find both the smallest and the largest numbers in the list since we can write:

```
1. ARRAY list(1:100)
2. LET index:=1
3. READ list(index)
4. LOOP WHILE list(index)<>0
5.    LET index:=index+1
6.    READ list(index)
```

```
7. REPEAT
8. LET length:=index-1
9. LET smallest:=list(1)
9a.LET largest:=list(1)
10.LOOP for index=2 to length
11.   IF list(index)<smallest
12.     THEN
13.        LET smallest:=list(index)
14.     ELSE
15.        IF list(index)>largest
15a.          THEN
15b.             LET largest:=list(index)
15c.          ELSE
15d.             SKIP
15e.        IFEND
16.   IFEND
17.REPEAT
18.PRINT smallest;largest
20.END
```

See how easy it is to amend the logical program and hence the resulting program to run on your computer.

Flushed with success we can now take our program even further by amending it to find not only the largest and the smallest in a list but also their sum and their average. We have already written a routine to calculate the sum and average of a set of numbers so all we have to do is to graft this onto our existing program as follows:

```
1. ARRAY list(1:100)
2. LET index:=1
3. READ list(index)
4. LOOP WHILE list(index)<>0
5.    LET index:=index+1
6.    READ list(index)
7. REPEAT
8. LET length:=index-1
9. LET smallest:=list(1)
9a.LET largest:=list(1)
9b.LET total:=list(1)
10.LOOP for index=2 to length
11.   IF list(index)<smallest
12.     THEN
13.        LET smallest:=list(index)
14.     ELSE
15.        IF list(index)>largest
15a.          THEN
15b.             LET largest:=list(index)
15c.          ELSE
15d.             SKIP
15e.        IFEND
16.   IFEND
17.   LET total:=total+list(index)
18.REPEAT
19.PRINT smallest;largest
20.LET average:=total/length
21.PRINT average;total
22.END
```

Notice that we have set the total of the numbers, as well as the largest and smallest, to the first number in the list and we have no need to count the numbers as they are processed because we have already done that as we read the numbers into the list at the start of the program. The conversion of the logical programs into your own version of BASIC is left to you. Do not forget to draw up a data table before you write the program.

## Example 4—A simple sort routine.

With this example we are going to put an existing program to good use. The program is the one in which we found the smallest in a list of numbers. In itself this is not really of great use but when put into another context it can be a very valuable piece of programming. What we are going to do is to use our piece of program to help us to sort a list of numbers into numerical order. We do this by first of all finding the smallest number in the list, which we can already do, then the next smallest, then the next, and so on, until finally we have pulled out the numbers from the list in numerical order. So here is our program again:

```
1.  ARRAY list(1:100)
2.  LET index:=1
3.  READ list(index)
4.  LOOP WHILE list(index)<>0
5.     LET index:=index+1
6.     READ list(index)
7.  REPEAT
8.  LET length:=index-1
9.  LET smallest:=list(1)
10.LOOP for index=2 to length
11.    IF list(index)<smallest
12.       THEN
13.          LET smallest:=list(index)
14.       ELSE
15.          SKIP
16.    IFEND
17.REPEAT
18.PRINT smallest
19.END
```

The first six lines of our program are going to be untouched since we must have our list ready to hold in memory prior to being sorted. Using our program to find the smallest in the list will certainly give us the first number in the sorted list, but how are we going to use it to find the next smallest, the next smallest, and so on ? We have to work out a strategy for the problem in such a way that we can use our ready-made routine. We can do this by saying that we will look for numbers which are the smallest so far but larger than the last number recorded in our numerical listing. In other words we will:

1. Read in the unsorted list.

2. Find the smallest number in the list and print it.
3. Loop until the printed list is the same length as the unsorted list.
4. Find the smallest number in the list greater than the last-smallest and print it.
5. Repeat.
6. End.

At first sight that seems fairly satisfactory and there is no doubt that we could work on the idea and produce a perfectly satisfactory program. But notice that we are in fact repeating ourselves in lines 2 and 4. Would it not be far better to somehow condense our program and use the routine once only? We could do this by initializing the last-smallest to a very low number, say −9999; and then we would get:

1. Read in the unsorted list.
2. Set the last-smallest to −9999.
3. Loop until the printed list is the same length as the unsorted list.
4. Find the smallest number in the list greater than the last-smallest and print it.
5. Repeat.
6. End.

It will be easy to find how the number of sorted numbers printed so far matches the length of the unsorted list because we have already had to find the value of **length** and we can then count the numbers as they are printed.

```
1.  ARRAY list(1:100)
2.  LET index:=1
3.  READ list(index)
4.  LOOP WHILE list(index)<>0
5.     LET index:=index+1
6.     READ list(index)
7.  REPEAT
8.  LET length:=index-1
9.  LET last:=-9999
10. LET count:=0
11. LOOP
12.    LET smallest:=9999
13.    LOOP for index=1 to length
14.       IF list(index)<smallest AND
             list(index)>last
15.          THEN
16.             LET smallest:=list(index)
17.          ELSE
18.             SKIP
19.       IFEND
20.    REPEAT
21.    LET count:=count+1
22.    PRINT smallest
23.    LET last:=smallest
24. REPEAT UNTIL count=length
25. END
```

Note how we have had to change lines 12 and 13. The reason for this is that there is always a possibility of the smallest number being the first in the list—at some time it is bound to be—so we set **smallest** to a high number (9999 in this case) every time round and take our loop from **index** values starting at one. We are now in a position to attempt a program to run on our computer. But first of all we need our data table:

| Logical Name | Purpose | Type | BASIC variable name |
|---|---|---|---|
| **list** | list of numbers | numeric array index (1:100) | L |
| **index** | index to **list** | integer | INDEX |
| **length** | length of **list** | integer | LENGTH% |
| **smallest** | smallest number | real | SMALL |
| **last** | previous smallest number | real | LAST |
| **count** | number of sorted numbers printed | integer | COUNT% |

We can then write this in BASIC:

```
10 DIM L(100)
20 INDEX%=1
30 INPUT L(INDEX%)
40 IF L(INDEX%)=0 THEN GOTO 70
50 INDEX%=INDEX%+1
60 GOTO 30
70 LENGTH%=INDEX%-1
80 LAST=-9999
90 COUNT%=0
100 SMALL=9999
110 FOR INDEX%=1 TO LENGTH%
120 IF L(INDEX%)<SMALL AND L(INDEX%)>LAST THEN SMALL=L(INDEX%)
130 NEXT INDEX%
140 COUNT%=COUNT%+1
150 PRINT SMALL
160 LAST=SMALL
```

```
170 IF COUNT%<>LENGTH% THEN GOTO 100
180 END
```

Another version of this in a BASIC which allows the use of WHILE is shown below. Notice again how all the GOTO statements are lost and the whole program is far easier to understand.

```
10 DIM L(100)
20 INDEX%=1
30 INPUT L(INDEX%)
40 WHILE L(INDEX%)<>0
50    INDEX%=INDEX%+1
60    INPUT L(INDEX%)
70 WEND
80 LENGTH%=INDEX%-1
90 LAST=-9999
100 COUNT%=0
110 WHILE COUNT%<>LENGTH%
120    SMALL=9999
130    FOR INDEX%=1 TO LENGTH%
140    IF L(INDEX%)<SMALL AND L(INDEX%)>LAST THEN SMALL=L(INDEX%)
150    NEXT INDEX%
160    COUNT%=COUNT%+1
170    PRINT SMALL
180    LAST=SMALL
190 WEND
200 END
```

This program works quite satisfactorily except for one thing, and that is going to be left to you, the reader, to rectify. It is that the program works for all the usual test procedures except one, which is perhaps one which you would not have thought of by yourself unless you spent a long time checking all the possible ways in which the data could be presented to the program. Try the effect of getting the program to sort a set of numbers which are (1) in reverse order, such as 99,98,97,96,95,...,(2) already in numerical order,(3) in any jumbled order, (4) in jumbled order but with repeated numbers, and finally (5) with all the numbers the same.

## Example 5—Merging

This example shows how we can develop a program which will merge the contents of two files into one file. This is a very common requirement in data processing. We very often have two files sorted into either numerical or alphabetical order and we need to create one new file from the two, which again will be in numerical or alphabetical order. For example, if the records in one of the files are referenced by 'keys'—in this case a numerical key—they could be a file of spare parts for a car—which could be the part number. The rest of the record for that part number could be its description, cost price, selling

**32**

price, number in stock, and so on. The records in the file to be merged with it could refer to changes in the status of any part, new parts to be added to the list, additions and withdrawals of stock, or changes in price. The two files have to be merged and a new, updated, file produced in numerical order of part numbers. For example, if one file consisted of the following records:

| Key (Part No) | Record |
|---|---|
| 12435 | ..................... |
| 12564 | ..................... |
| 12576 | ..................... |
| 12675 | ..................... |
| 12678 | ..................... |
| etc. | |

and the other file contained records such as

| KEY (Part no) | Record |
|---|---|
| 12436 | details of a new part |
| 12576 | amended details of part |
| 12577 | details of a new part |
| 12678 | amended details of part |
| etc. | |

then the new merged file could look like:

| KEY (Part no) | Record |
|---|---|
| 12435 | unchanged record |
| 12436 | details of new part |
| 12564 | unchanged record |
| 12576 | amended record |
| 12577 | details of new part |
| 12675 | unchanged record |
| 12678 | amended record |

Our first attempt at deciding on a plan is this:

1. Initialize all files.
2. Read first key from each file.
3. Loop while there are unread records on both files.
4. Place the record with the smaller key onto the new file.

5. Read the next record from the file which provided the last record written.
6. Repeat.
7. Place the remaining records onto the new file.

The thing to remember is that the two files will almost certainly be of unequal lengths. This means that the end of one file will be reached before the end of the other is reached. The unread records remaining are then read without alteration onto the new file since there are no records remaining on the other file to compare them with. So let us refine this, bearing the last point in mind.

1. Initialize all files.
2. Read record from each file; call keys P and Q.
3. Loop while there are records on both files.
4.    If P<Q
5.       Then
6.          Write record(P) to output file.
7.          Read next record from file providing record(P).
8.       Else
9.          Write record(Q) to output file.
10.         Read next record from file providing record(Q)
11.    Ifend.
12.Repeat.
13.Loop while there are records on the remaining file.
14.    Write record to output file.
15.    Read record from input file.
16.Repeat.
17.End.

But there is a snag. If you look at the list of entries in the two files you should notice that some entries have the same key and our design does not allow for that. So before we go any further we have to put in a section of program which takes this situation into account. Because of the way we have designed the program such an amendment is easy to make. Note that if two records have the same key we only write the more up-to-date record to the new file and then read two new records. Incidentally, 'initializing' a file does not mean setting it to zero. It means that the computer is made aware that files are to be used on disk or tape. Another term used is 'open a file'.

1. Initialize all files.

2. Read record from each file; call keys P and Q.
3. Loop while there are records on both files.
3a.　　If P=Q
3b.　　Then
3c.　　　　Write record(P) to output file.
3d.　　　　Read next record from each file.
3e.　　Else
4.　　　　If P<Q
5.　　　　Then
6.　　　　　　Write record(P) to output file
7.　　　　　　Read next record from file providing record(P).
8.　　　　Else
9.　　　　　　Write record(Q) to output file.
10.　　　　　Read next record from file providing record(Q).
11.　　　Ifend.
11a.　　Ifend.
12. Repeat.
13. Loop while there are records on the remaining file.
14.　　Write record to output file.
15.　　Read record from input file.
16. Repeat.
17. End.

Notice the order of things in lines 14 and 15. We have to write the current record before we read the next one. Otherwise we shall lose the last record on the file. Now it is beginning to get somewhere, so we must start being rather more specific. We will call the two input files by the names "A" and "B" and the output file by the name "C". In addition we have to allocate channels to each file—logical numbers if you like. This is because we usually reference files not by name but by the channel of communication we establish with them. The actual initializing of files sets up the relationship between the name of the file and the channel we reach it by. It is rather like saying that we take the route along the M1 rather than the Birmingham road.

1. Initialize all files:#1 to "A",#2 to "B" #3 to "C".
2. Read first record on #1.
3. Let P:=record key.
4. Read first record on #2.
5. Let Q:=record key.
6. Loop while there are records unread in "A" and "B".
7.　　If P=Q
8.　　Then
9.　　　　Write record(key P) to #3.

10.        Read next record on #1.
11.        Read next record on #2.
12.   Else
13.     If $P<Q$
14.     Then
15.        Write record(key P) to #3.
16.        Read next record on #1.
17.        Set P:=record key.
18.     Else
19.        Write record(key Q) on #3.
20.        Read next record on #2.
21.        Set Q:=record key.
22.   Ifend.
23.  Ifend.
24.Repeat.
25.If end of "A" found first
26.  Then
27.     Loop while there are unread records on "B".
28.        Write record on #3.
29.        Read next record on #2.
30.     Repeat.
31.  Else
32.     Loop while there are unread records on "A".
33.        Write record on #3.
34.        Read next record on #1.
35.     Repeat.
29.  Ifend.
30. End.

We can refine this even more by putting it in pseudo-code:

```
1.    OPEN file "A" on #1 for reading
2.    OPEN file "B" on #2 for reading
3.    OPEN file "C" on #3 for writing
4.    READ record on #1
5.    LET P:=key(record)
6.    READ record on #2
7.    LET Q:=key(record)
8.    LOOP WHILE records remain to be read on #1 and #2
9.       IF P=Q
10.        THEN
11.           WRITE record(P) on #3
12.           READ record on #1
13.           LET P:=key(record)
14.           READ record on #2
15.           LET Q:=key(record)
16.        ELSE
17.           IF P<Q
18.              THEN
19.                 WRITE record(P) on #3
20.                 READ record on #1
21.                 LET P:=key(record)
```

```
22.        ELSE
23.            WRITE record(Q) in #3
24.            READ record on #2
25.            LET Q:=key(record)
26.        IFEND
27.    IFEND
28.  REPEAT
29.  IF end of file"A" reached
30.    THEN
31.      LOOP WHILE there are records on "B"
32.        WRITE record on #3
33.        READ record on #2
34.      REPEAT
35.    ELSE
36.      LOOP WHILE there are records on "A"
37.        WRITE record on #3
38.        READ record on #1
39.      REPEAT
40.  IFEND
41. END
```

We are now in a position to write the program in BASIC and for this example we are going to provide several versions. The first of these is useful if one has a disk drive on which the three files can be stored. But first our data table:

| Logical name | Purpose | Type | BASIC variable name |
| --- | --- | --- | --- |
| A | file of records | sequential file | A |
| B | file of records | sequential file | B |
| C | file of records | sequential file | C |
| **record** | record from a file | string | P$ — from "A"<br>Q$ — from "B" |
| P | keys to **records** | real | P — from "A" |
| Q | | | Q — from "B" |

```
10 OPEN "I",1,"A"
20 OPEN "I",2,"B"
30 OPEN "O",3,"C"
40 INPUT#1,P$
50 P=VAL(LEFT$(P$,5))
60 INPUT#2,Q$
70 Q=VAL(LEFT$(Q$,5))
80 IF EOF(1) THEN GOTO 310 ELSE IF EOF(2) THEN GOTO 360
90 IF P<>Q THEN GOTO 170
```

```
110 PRINT#3,P$
120 INPUT#1,P$
130 P=VAL(LEFT$(P$,5))
140 INPUT#2,Q$
150 Q=VAL(LEFT$(Q$,5))
160 GOTO 80
170 IF P>Q THEN GOTO 230
190 PRINT#3,P$
200 INPUT#1,P$
210 P=VAL(LEFT$(P$,5))
220 GOTO 80
230 PRINT#3,Q$
240 INPUT#2,Q$
250 Q=VAL(LEFT$(Q$,5))
260 GOTO 80
310 IF EOF(2) THEN STOP
320 PRINT#3,Q$
330 INPUT#2,Q$
340 GOTO 310
360 IF EOF(1) THEN STOP
370 PRINT#3,P$
380 INPUT#1,P$
390 GOTO 360
```

Not everyone is going to have a computer with disk storage available. In fact, there are going to be many people who want to learn about programming who only have a microcomputer with a single cassette tape unit. This does not affect the use of this program at all. It merely means that we have to approach the coding in a slightly different way because of the different facilities available. What we do is to read one of the files into memory first and store it there as a list. We then read off this list, record by record, just as we would read from a disk file. We are still reading and processing one record at a time so the main part of the program is unaltered. All we have to do is make a little adjustment first of all to read the file "A" into memory and store it as a list called A. Successive records of the file will be indexed just as with any other list. We will read the file "B" from our tape just as before and assemble the amended file, called "C" previously, into another list held in memory called C. Finally we will write the list C onto a new file on tape which we will call "C". So to start with we will get:

1. Initialize #1 to "A".
2. Reserve 100 locations in memory for list **A**.
3. Initialize **index** to 1.
4. Loop while there are records on "A".
5.    Read record from #1.
6.    Let **A**(**index**):=record.
7.    Let **index**:=**index**+1.
8. Repeat.
9. Let **length**:=number of records read into **A**.
10. Close #1.

11. Initialize #1 to "**B**".
12. Reserve 200 locations in memory for list **C**.
13. Let **index**:=1.
14. Let **count**:=1.
15. Let **P**:=record key of **A**(**index**).
16. Read first record on #1.
17. Let **Q**:=record key.
18. Loop while there are records unread on "**B**" or **index>length**.
19.   If **P**=**Q**
20.     Then
21.         Let **C**(**count**):=**A**(**index**).
22.         Let **count**:=**count**+1.
23.         Let **index**:=**index**+1
24.         Let **P**:=key(**A**(**index**)).
25.         Read next record on #1.
26.         Let **Q**:=key(**Q**).
27.     Else
28.         If **P**<**Q**
29.           Then
30.               Let **C**(**count**):=**A**(**index**).
31.               Let **count**:=**count**+1.
32.               Let **index**:=**index**+1.
33.               Let **P**:= key(**A**(**index**)).
34.           Else
35.               Let **C**(**count**):=record key(**Q**).
36.               Let **count**:=**count**+1.
37.               Read next record on #1.
38.               Set **Q**:=record key.
39.         Ifend.
40.     Ifend.
41. Repeat.
42. If last record in **A** has been read
43.   Then
44.       Let **C**(**count**):=record key(**Q**).
45.       Let **count**:=**count**+1.
46.       Loop while there are unread records on "**B**".
47.           Read next record on #1.
48.           Let **C**(**count**):=record.
49.           Let **count**:=**count**+1.
50.       Repeat.
51.   Else
52.       Let **C**(**count**):=**A**(**index**).
53.       Loop while **index** >**length**.

54.      Let **C(count):=A(index)**.
55.      Let **count:=count+1**.
56.      Let **index:=index+1**.
57.    Repeat.
58.Ifend.
59.Close #1.
60.Initialize #1 to "**C**".
61.Loop for **check**   1 to **count**-1.
62.   Write **C(check)** to #1.
63.Repeat.
64.End.

In order to code this in BASIC we can have a program which looks as follows. It is written in Commodore BASIC and was run on a Vic-20 home computer with a single cassette drive. Notice that there have to be points in the program where the program stops in order for the user to change cassettes and to press the 'record' and 'play' keys on the recorder when the final merged list file is written to the file called "C". We first need the data table:

| Logical Name | Purpose | Type | BASIC variable name |
|---|---|---|---|
| **A** | list of records | string array index (1:100) | A$ |
| **B** | file of records | sequential file | B |
| **C** | list of records | string array index (1:200) | C$ |
| **P** | key to record in **A** | real | P |
| **Q** | key to record in **B** | real | Q |

**40**

| index | index to list A | integer | INDEX% |
|-------|-----------------|---------|--------|
| length | number of records in A | integer | L% |
| count | index to list C | integer | COUNT% |
| check | index to list C on print to file | integer | CHECK% |

## This can be written in BASIC:

```
10 OPEN 1,1,0,"A"
20 DIM A$(100)
30 INDEX%=1
40 INPUT#1,P$
50 IF ST=64 THEN GOTO 90
60 A$(INDEX%)=P$
70 INDEX%=INDEX%+1
80 GOTO 40
90 A$(INDEX%)=P$
100 L%=INDEX%
112 CLOSE 1
114 PRINT"NOW STOP THE TAPE"
120 STOP
130 OPEN 1,1,0,"B"
140 INDEX%=1
150 COUNT%=1
160 DIM C$(200)
170 P=VAL(LEFT$(A$(INDEX%),5))
180 INPUT#1,Q$
190 Q=VAL(LEFT$(Q$,5))
200 IF INDEX%>L% THEN GOTO 420
210 IF P<>Q THEN GOTO 300
220 C$(COUNT%)=A$(INDEX%)
230 COUNT%=COUNT%+1
240 INDEX%=INDEX%+1
250 P=VAL(LEFT$(A$(INDEX%),5))
260 INPUT#1,Q$
270 IF ST=64 THEN GOTO 480
280 Q=VAL(LEFT$(Q$,5))
290 GOTO 200
300 IF P>Q THEN GOTO 360
310 C$(COUNT%)=A$(INDEX%)
320 COUNT%=COUNT%+1
330 INDEX%=INDEX%+1
340 P=VAL(LEFT$(A$(INDEX%),5))
350 GOTO 200
360 C$(COUNT%)=Q$
370 COUNT%=COUNT%+1
380 INPUT#1,Q$
390 IF ST=64 THEN GOTO 480
```

```
400 Q=VAL(LEFT$(Q$,5))
410 GOTO 200
420 C$(COUNT%)=Q$
430 COUNT%=COUNT%+1
440 INPUT#1,Q$
450 IF ST=64 THEN GOTO 480
460 C$(COUNT%)=Q$
470 COUNT%=COUNT%+1
460 GOTO 440
480 C$(COUNT%)=A$(INDEX%)
490 IF INDEX%> L% THEN GOTO 540
500 C$(COUNT%)=A$(INDEX%)
510 COUNT%=COUNT%+1
520 INDEX%=INDEX%+1
530 GOTO 490
540 CLOSE 1
542 PRINT"NOW STOP THE TAPE"
544 STOP
550 OPEN 1,1,1,"C"
560 FOR CHECK%=1 TO COUNT%-1
570 PRINT#1,C$(CHECK%)
580 NEXT CHECK%
590 CLOSE 1
600 END
```

# Example 6—Subprograms

This example shows the use of subroutines or subprograms which are called upon by a main program as and when they are needed. In other words, if we write a program needing a routine to be executed which is really nothing to do with the main stream of the program then any such routine can be written separately from the main program, and can even be tested on its own before being incorporated into the program which uses it. Such routines are called **subroutines** or **procedures**. To illustrate the concept we will write a program by which we can perform currency conversion from pounds sterling to or from any other currency. So we will write:

1. Loop.
2. Ask for currency to be converted.
3. Ask for the rate of exchange.
4. Ask if to or from sterling.
5. If from sterling then perform the appropriate conversion.
6. If to sterling perform the appropriate conversion.
7. Repeat until there are no more conversions to perform.

We can refine this to become:

```
1. LOOP
2.     READ currency$
3.     READ rate
4.     READ direction$
```

42

```
5.    IF direction$="to"
6.       THEN
7.          EXECUTE "TOSTERLING"
8.       ELSE
9.          EXECUTE "FROMSTERLING"
10.   IFEND
11.READ more$
12.REPEAT UNTIL more$="no"
13.END
```

Both of the subprograms need to know the name of the currency and the rate of exchange so we have to transfer these to the routines. They then have some data to work on and then can calculate and print the answer for us. The information transferred to the routine is called the **parameters of the routine** and we should really write our program as follows:

```
1.LOOP
2.    READ currency$
3.    READ rate
4.    READ direction$
5.    IF direction$="to"
6.       THEN
7.          EXECUTE "TOSTERLING"(currency$,rate)
8.       ELSE
9.          EXECUTE "FROMSTERLING"(currency$,rate)
10.   IFEND
11.   READ more$
12.REPEAT UNTIL more$="no"
13.END
```

where we have placed the names of the variables whose values we want to transfer to the subprograms called TOSTERLING and FROMSTERLING. Thus we can construct our subprograms as follows:

```
SUBPROGRAM TOSTERLING(currency$,rate)
1.  PRINT "How many "; currency$ ;"?"
2.  READ amount
3.  LET value:=amount/rate
4.  PRINT amount;currency$;"=";value;"Pounds Sterling"
END OF SUBPROGRAM
```

and:

```
SUBPROGRAM FROMSTERLING(currency$,rate)
1.  PRINT "How many pounds ?"
2.  READ amount
3.  LET value=amount*rate
4.  PRINT amount;"Pounds Sterling =";value,currency$
END OF SUBPROGRAM
```

**43**

First we need the data table:

| Logical Name | Purpose | Type | BASIC variable name |
|---|---|---|---|
| **more$** | controls request for more calculations | string | MORE$ |
| **currency$** | name of currency | string | CURRENCY$ |
| **rate** | rate of exchange | real | RATE |
| **direction$** | selection of subroutine | string | DIRECTION$ |
| **amount** | amount of money | real | AMOUNT |
| **value** | converted value | real | VALUE |

Now let us write the program in conventional BASIC where we again use two subroutines to do our conversions:

```
10 INPUT CURRENCY$
20 INPUT RATE
30 INPUT DIRECTION$
40 IF DIRECTION$="TO" THEN GOSUB 80 ELSE GOSUB 130
50 INPUT MORE$
60 IF MORE$="NO" THEN STOP ELSE GOTO 10
70 PRINT "HOW MANY";CURRENCY$;"?"
80 INPUT AMOUNT
90 VALUE=AMOUNT/RATE
100 PRINT AMOUNT;CURRENCY$;"=";VALUE;"POUNDS STERLING"
110 RETURN
120 PRINT "HOW MANY POUNDS ?"
130 INPUT AMOUNT
140 VALUE = AMOUNT*RATE
150 PRINT AMOUNT;"POUNDS STERLING =";VALUE;CURRENCY$
160 RETURN
```

If this is written in BBC BASIC we can use a **procedure** instead of a subroutine. Notice that we define a procedure and give it an identifing name, T or F for our example, and that we place the values of the parameters to be used in the procedure in

**44**

brackets after its name:

```
10 REPEAT
20    INPUT CURRENCY$
30    INPUT RATE
40    INPUT DIRECTION$
50    IF DIRECTION$="TO" THEN PROCT(CURRENCY$,RATE) ELSE PROCF(CURRENCY$,RATE
60    INPUT MORE$
70 UNTIL MORE$="NO"
80 END
90 DEF PROCT(CURRENCY$,RATE)
100 INPUT AMOUNT
110 MONEY=AMOUNT/RATE
120 PRINT AMOUNT;CURRENCY$;"=";MONEY;"POUNDS STERLING"
130 ENDPROC
140 DEF PROCF(CURRENCY$,RATE)
150 PRINT "HOW MANY POUNDS ?"
160 INPUT AMOUNT
170 MONEY=AMOUNT*RATE
180 PRINT AMOUNT;"POUNDS STERLING =";MONEY;CURRENCY$
190 ENDPROC
```

## Example 7—More sorting

The topic of sorting data has already been touched on in a previous example when the technique known as 'replacement selection' was used. Here is another method of sorting which can be applied to data stored in a file or in memory equally well. It is usually called a 'bubble' sort.

Imagine a set of numbers, or names for that matter, arranged in a list which are scanned from left to right in such a way that each adjacent pair of data items are compared and exchanged if the one on the left is larger—or higher in the alphabet—than the one on the right. They are left alone if the one on the left is already the smaller of the pair. By the time the entire list has been scanned once the largest number will have 'bubbled' up to the extreme right hand end of the list. The list is then rescanned and the second largest will take its rightful place before the largest and so on. Eventually the entire list has been placed in order. Successive versions of the list will be as shown below:

34,65,23,19,17,20

After the first scan we will have:

34,23,19,17,20,65

**45**

then

23,19,17,20,34,65

then

19,17,20,23,34,65

and finally

17,19,20,23,34,65

So if we design a method of sorting using this technique we would write:

1. Read the numbers into a list.
2. Start with the first pair of numbers; if the first exceeds the second exchange them. If not leave them alone.
3. Repeat the operation in 2 for the next pair until we reach the end of the list.
4. Go back to the beginning of the list and repeat the operation until all the numbers have been sorted.

We have already written the first step in a previous example. The other steps perhaps ought to be written as:

2. Loop.
3. Start at the beginning of the list and compare pairs of adjacent entries. If the first of the pair exceeds the second exchange them. Otherwise do nothing.
4. Repeat until the list has been sorted.

In pseudo-code this starts off as:

```
1. ARRAY list(1:100)
2. LET index:=1
3. READ list(index)
4. LOOP WHILE list(index)<>0
5.    LET index:=index+1
6.    READ list(index)
7. REPEAT
8. LET length:=index-1
```

and we will have the numbers stored in a list ready to be sorted. Then we have to test pairs of numbers starting from the beginning of the list. So we can say:

```
9.  LOOP WHILE the list is unsorted.
10.   LOOP FOR  index=1 TO length-1
11.     IF list(index)>list(index+1)
12.       THEN
13         EXCHANGE list(index) and list(index+1)
14.       ELSE
15.         SKIP
16.     IFEND
17.   REPEAT
18.REPEAT
```

This now leaves us with two problems to solve. The first of these is to devise a means by which we can tell when the list has been sorted; the second is to decide how we will exchange a pair of numbers held in memory. We will deal with the second problem first as in fact it leads us to the solution of the first problem.

In order to exchange the contents of two memory locations we actually need a third. This acts as temporary storage in the same way as we need a third temporary container if we want to exchange the contents of two glasses. We need to pour the contents of one glass into a third glass, i.e.,

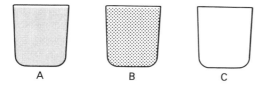

In order to place the contents of A into B and B into A we first pour the contents of A into C, the empty glass:

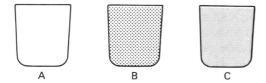

Then we pour the contents of B into A:

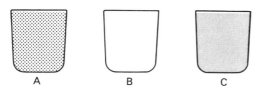

and the contents of C into B:

**47**

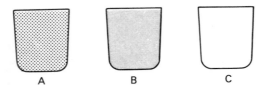

A        B        C

The EXCHANGE routine becomes:

```
13a.  LET temp:=list(index)
13b.  LET list(index):=list(index+1)
13c.  LET list(index+1):=temp
```

Now we can see how to tell if our list has been sorted since we can place a 'flag' or marker in the EXCHANGE part of the program which tells us if an exchange has been made. If we can scan completely through the list without an exchange being made the list must be sorted. So we add an extra line to the end of EXCHANGE:

```
13d.  LET flag:=1
```

and an extra line before the start of the loop to set **flag** to zero. We then can amend lines 9 and 18 to give:

```
9.LOOP
```

together with:

```
18.  REPEAT UNTIL flag=0
```

since we are looking for a situation where on emerging from the EXCHANGE routine the value of **flag** is zero, indicating that no exchanges have been made. So we must reset the value of **flag** to zero before we enter EXCHANGE:

```
9a.  LET flag:=0
```

The complete program will then look like this:

```
1.  ARRAY list(1:100)
2.  LET index:=1
3.  READ list(index)
4.  LOOP WHILE list(index)<>0
5.      LET index:=index+1
6.      READ list(index)
7.  REPEAT
8.  LET length:=index-1
9.  LOOP
```

**48**

```
9a    LET flag:=0
10.   LOOP FOR   index=1 TO length-1
11.      IF list(index))>list(index+1)
12.         THEN
13a.           LET temp:=list(index)
13b.           LET list(index):=list(lindex+1)
13c.           LET list(index+1):=temp
13d.           LET flag:=1
14.      ELSE
15.          SKIP
16.      IFEND
17.   REPEAT
18.REPEAT UNTIL flag=0
19.LOOP FOR index=1 to length
20.   PRINT list(index)
21.REPEAT
22.END
```

One more improvement can be made on the code between lines 10 and 17 where we are scanning through the whole of the list every time. This is not really necessary and is very time consuming if we are sorting a very long list since we know that the sorted part of the list is continually becoming longer and longer and in that part of the list we are performing tests which are not needed. If we only scan the unsorted part of the list each time we are going to end up with a much more efficient program. What we need to do is to reduce the number of pairs of numbers tested by one each time we traverse the list. This means an amendment to line 10 so that we go to **length**-1, **length**-2, **length**-3 and so on. Two new lines and a change to line 10 will do this:

```
9b.LET n:=1
10.LOOP FOR index=1 TO length-n
17a.LET n:=n+1
```

## and so we get:

```
1.   ARRAY list(1:100)
2.   LET index:=1
3.   READ list(index)
4.   LOOP WHILE list(index)<>0
5.      LET index:=index+1
6.      READ list(index)
7.   REPEAT
8.   LET length:=index-1
9.   LOOP
9a     LET flag:=0
9b.    LET n:=1
10.    LOOP FOR index=1 TO length-n
11.       IF list(index)>list(index+1)
12.          THEN
13a.            LET temp:=list(index)
13b.            LET list(index):=list(lindex+1)
13c.            LET list(index+1):=temp
13d.            LET flag:=1
14.       ELSE
15.           SKIP
```

```
16.    IFEND
17.  REPEAT
17a. LET n:=n+1
18.REPEAT UNTIL flag=0
19.LOOP FOR index=1 to length
20.   PRINT list(index)
21.REPEAT
22.END
```

Now we can produce a data table:

| Logical Name | Purpose | Type | BASIC variable name |
|---|---|---|---|
| **list** | list of numbers | numeric array index (1:100) | L |
| **index** | index to **list** | integer | INDEX% |
| **length** | length of **list** | integer | LENGTH% |
| **temp** | temporary storage | real | TEMP |
| **n** | controller for loop | real | N |
| **flag** | flag for sort complete | real | FLAG |

A BASIC program, using WHILE, looks like this:

```
10 DIM L(100)
20 INDEX%=1
30 INPUT L(INDEX%)
40 WHILE L(INDEX%)<>0
50   INDEX%=INDEX%+1
60   INPUT L(INDEX%)
70 WEND
80 LENGTH%=INDEX%-1
90 N=1
100 FLAG=0
110 FOR INDEX%=1 TO LENGTH%-N
120   IF L(INDEX%)>L(INDEX%+1) THEN GOSUB 200
130 NEXT INDEX%
140   N=N+1
150 IF FLAG = 1 THEN GOTO 100
160 FOR INDEX%=1 TO LENGTH%
170   PRINT L(INDEX%)
180 NEXT INDEX%
190 END
```

```
200 TEMP=L(INDEX%)
210 L(INDEX%)=L(INDEX%+1)
220 L(INDEX%+1)=TEMP
230 FLAG=1
240 RETURN
```

whereas if we have REPEAT...UNTIL and the PROCedures
facility we could write:

```
10 DIM L(100)
20 INDEX%=0
40 REPEAT
50    INDEX%=INDEX%+1
60    INPUT L(INDEX%)
70 UNTIL L(INDEX%)=0
80 NUMBER%=INDEX%-1
90 N=1
95 REPEAT
100    FLAG=0
110    FOR INDEX%=1 TO NUMBER%-N
120       IF L(INDEX%)>L(INDEX%+1) THEN PROCA(L,INDEX%)
130    NEXT INDEX%
140    N=N+1
150 UNTIL FLAG=0
160 FOR INDEX%=1 TO NUMBER%
170    PRINT L(INDEX%)
180 NEXT INDEX%
190 END
195 DEF PROCA(L,INDEX%)
200 TEMP=L(INDEX%)
210 L(INDEX%)=L(INDEX%+1)
220 L(INDEX%+1)=TEMP
230 FLAG=1
240 ENDPROC
```

The above programs are suitable for sorting a list of numbers
into numerical order. Should we need to sort a list of names into
alphabetical order we can modify the program very easily by
changing the variables into strings by the addition of the $ sign
after their names so that we get:

| Logical Name | Purpose | Type | BASIC variable name |
|---|---|---|---|
| **list$** | list of names | string array index (1:100) | L$ |
| **index** | index to **list$** | integer | INDEX% |
| **length** | length of **list$** | integer | LENGTH% |
| **temp$** | temporary storage | real | TEMP$ |

| | | | |
|---|---|---|---|
| **n** | controller for loop | real | N |
| **flag** | flag for sort complete | real | FLAG |

One of the BASIC programs would be:

```
10 DIM L$(100)
20 INDEX%=1
30 INPUT L$(INDEX%)
40 WHILE L$(INDEX%)<>0
50    INDEX%=INDEX%+1
60    INPUT L$(INDEX%)
70 WEND
80 LENGTH%=INDEX%-1
90 N=1
100 FLAG=0
110 FOR INDEX%=1 TO LENGTH%-N
120    IF L$(INDEX%)>L$(INDEX%+1) THEN GOSUB 200
130 NEXT INDEX%
140    N=N+1
150 IF FLAG = 1 THEN GOTO 100
160 FOR INDEX%=1 TO LENGTH%
170    PRINT L$(INDEX%)
180 NEXT INDEX%
190 END
200 TEMP$=L$(INDEX%)
210 L$(INDEX%)=L$(INDEX%+1)
220 L$(INDEX%+1)=TEMP$
230 FLAG=1
240 RETURN
```

This may not be the fastest method of sorting a list of names or numbers but it is easy to understand. Other methods which are rather more complex, and hence more difficult to follow, are the 'shuttle' sort, 'quicksort' and the 'shell' sort. Investigation of these could prove fruitful.

Having a computer with only a tape cassette unit forces all sorting to be done in memory, as the previous examples show. Such 'internal' sorting procedures are quite fast, depending on the method used, but are restricted by the size of memory available . If sorting is to be performed on very large amounts of data then a disk drive would be needed. As well as allowing us to use sorting techniques based on the methods already mentioned—of which there is an example later—a disk allows us to make use of some other very sophisticated sorting techniques, in particular a method called a 'polyphase sort' which uses serial files. To give some idea of the relative amounts of storage available in memory and on a disk, consider that many of the computers used in schools and small businesses commonly have a memory which will allow the storage of about fifty thousand characters— a 48K RAM—and a disk drive will be able to store at least one hundred thousand characters, and possibly several times that number. In addition, remember that the RAM of your computer has to be able to store not only the data being sorted but also the program which controls the sorting. Hence, to sort large quantities of data a disk drive is essential. This produces its own problems which are often unforeseen. This was brought home to the author when faced with the problem of sorting over 800 records into alphabetical order. The memory size available was just enough to get all the records into memory at once and a comparison was made between sorting in memory and a disk-based sort. The results were interesting. The in-memory sort took about 40 minutes while the sort on disk, using the same method except that records were swapped about on disk, instead of memory, took almost 4 hours! This just goes to show that whatever is said about microcomputers they are generally nothing like as fast in operation as their larger brothers.

However, we can get over these problems, although in a rather cumbersome way, by sorting sections of a file and then merging the sections into a new sorted file, as shown in one of the earlier examples. Nevertheless, the next example is shown for the benefit of those with a disk drive and is a program in BASIC which sorts a file using the 'bubble' sort technique used in the earlier part of this example. The method of sorting is exactly the same, but the coding for the BASIC program is such that it takes into account the features of Microsoft(TM) BASIC. The program looks like this:

```
5 REM***OPEN A RANDOM ACCESS FILE***
6 REM***EACH RECORD 40 CHARACTERS LONG***
10 OPEN "R",1,"RAND",40
15 REM***EACH RECORD CONTAINS ONE FIELD CALLED A$***
20 FIELD 1,40 AS A$
25 REM***R IS THE NO. OF RECORDS TO BE SORTED -1***
30 R=9
40 F=0
50 FOR I = 1 TO R
55 REM***READ THE Ith RECORD FROM THE FILE***
60 GET 1,I
65 REM***ALLOCATE THE STRING READ TO P1$***
70 P1$=A$
75 REM***READ THE (I+1)th RECORD FROM THE FILE***
80 GET 1,I+1
85 REM***ALLOCATE THE STRING READ TO P2$***
90 P2$=A$
95 REM***TEST FOR LARGER STRING***
100 IF P1$>P2$ THEN GOSUB 170
110 NEXT I
115 REM***AFTER A COMPLETE SCAN TEST FOR A SWAP***
116 REM***HAVING TAKEN PLACE***
120 IF F=0 THEN 150
130 R=R-1
140 GOTO 40
150 CLOSE
160 STOP
```

```
165 REM***REWRITE THE STRINGS READ INTO EACH***
166 REM***OTHER'S RECORD***
170 LSET A$=P2$
180 PUT 1,I
190 LSET A$=P1$
200 PUT 1,I+1
205 REM***SET SWAP FLAG***
210 F=1
220 RETURN
```

Notice that the sorting takes place on a file which is created as a random or 'direct' access file. You cannot do this if the file has been created and set up as a serial file. You cannot read from or write to specific records in a serial file. Such a file has to be read from or written to from the start right through to the finish. There are a number of methods of sorting the contents of disk files into order, but the one shown here is the easiest to understand and it works quite satisfactorily. However, the method becomes painfully slow using the minidisks supplied with many of the current microcomputers if large files are to be sorted. A way around the problem is to read just the keys and the record numbers into memory and sort them. Then the records can be read out according to the sorted keys. Once one becomes used to handling files on disk then there are many very clever ways of manipulating them, and these techniques are discussed in many of the standard books on computing science. This book gives, hopefully, ideas and provides an appetite to go on to more subtle things.

## Example 8—Searching

The topic of sorting data always goes hand in hand with that of searching for data. In other words, if we have to go and look for data held in a file, or a list, then it should be sorted first so that we can at least have some idea of where the required data are in the file before we start looking for them. If this is not done then searching for data becomes haphazard,time-consuming and very inefficient. There are numerous ways of searching for data which have already been arranged in, let us say, alphabetical order. For example, if we have a list of telephone numbers which is arranged in order of names then we need some method of searching for the name which matches the required name without having to search through the list from the start until we find the required name and its corresponding number.

We will start by solving a simpler problem so that we can get the method clearly fixed in our mind. Let us look at the problem of finding the position of a number from an ordered list. We have

**54**

a list of numbers such as:

3,5,6,8,9,10,12,14,17,18,21,23,34

we want a program which will allow us to input a number, say 10, and get the answer that 10 is sixth in the list. On the other hand, if we input the number 11 into the program we should get a message that 11 does not exist in the list. Our technique is really quite simple and consists of dividing the list into two parts, an upper half and a lower half. Then we decide in which half of the list our number resides. Next we divide that half into two further equal parts and discover the part in which our number now resides. We continue to do this with smaller and smaller sections of the list until we are left with a sublist one number long. Our input number either matches this single number, in which case we have found what we are looking for, or it does not, in which case we know that our search has failed. So let us write this down:

1. Read our numbers into a list.
2. Read in the number to be searched for.
3. Find the mid-point of the list.
4. Loop.
5. If the number read in equals the number at the mid-point then the number is found.
6. If the number read in exceeds the number at the mid-point then find the mid-point of the upper half of the range.
7. Else find the mid-point of the lower half of the range.
8. Repeat until the number is found.
9. Print "Number not found".

Let us expand the sequence from step 5; if we have found that the number being searched for matches the number at the current mid-point of our list, or sublist, then we have achieved our object and the program should stop. If we have not done this then, depending upon whether our number is higher or lower than the one held at that current mid-point, we start looking at a list half as long; so we have to redefine the start and finish of our new sublist. For example if our list is

4,6,7,9,11,15,17,20

and we are going to search for the position of the number 7 in that list then, there being eight numbers in the list, the mid-point is 4 (the integer result from dividing 8, the highest number position, plus 1, the lowest, by 2). The number in the fourth position is 9 and this is greater than the number we are searching for. This means that we can redefine the top of the list to be looked at now as 3—there is no point in including the fourth number as we know that it is too large anyway. So now we look at the new mid-point number, 6 in position 2; (CHOP((1+3)/2).That number is too small and so we replace the low marker by 3; (2+1) and look at the number held in position CHOP((3+3)/2), which is 3. The number there is the 7 we are looking for. Notice that we are successively reducing the length of each sublist until we have only one number contained in it. If that does not match then we will be forced to continue the sequence but will reach a position where the low marker exceeds the high marker, which is sufficient to tell us that we have failed to find the required number. Let us write that down in our pseudo-code:

```
1.  ARRAY list(1:100)
2.  LET index:=1
3.  READ list(index)
4.  LOOP WHILE list(index)<>0
5.     LET index=index+1
6.     READ list(index)
7.  REPEAT
8.  LET length=index-1
9.  READ number
10. LET lo:=1
11. LET hi:=length
12. LET mid:=CHOP((lo+hi)/2)
13. LOOP WHILE lo<=hi
14.    LET mid:=CHOP((lo+hi)/2)
15.    IF number=list(mid)
16.       THEN
17.          PRINT list(mid);"FOUND AT";mid
18.       ELSE
19.          IF number>list(mid)
20.             THEN
21.                LET lo:=mid+1
22.             ELSE
23.                LET hi:=mid-1
24.             IFEND
25.    IFEND
26. REPEAT
27. PRINT number;"not found"
28. END
```

Now for a data table:

| Logical Name | Purpose | Type | BASIC variable name |
|---|---|---|---|
| **list** | list of numbers | numeric array index (1:100) | L |

| index | index to list | integer | INDEX% |
|---|---|---|---|
| length | length of list | integer | LENGTH% |
| number | number being searched for | real | N |
| lo | index of bottom of sublist | integer | LO% |
| hi | index of top of sublist | integer | HI% |
| mid | mid-point index of sublist | integer | MID% |

We will now write the program in BASIC using the WHILE statement. It will be a useful test of your command of your version of the language for you to convert it to a program which will run on your computer.

```
10 DIM L(100)
20 INDEX%=1
30 INPUT L(INDEX%)
40 WHILE L(INDEX%)<>0
50    INDEX%=INDEX%+1
60    INPUT L(INDEX%)
70 WEND
80 LENGTH%=INDEX%-1
90 INPUT N
100 LO%=1
110 HI%=LENGTH%
120 MID%=INT(LO%+HI%)/2)
130 WHILE LO%<=HI%
140    MID%=INT(LO%+HI%)/2)
150    IF N=L(MID%)  THEN GOTO 190
           ELSE IF N>L(MID%) THEN LO%=MID%+1 ELSE HI%=MID%-1
160 WEND
170 PRINT N;"not found"
180 STOP
190 PRINT L(MID%);"FOUND AT";MID%
200 STOP
```

It might be worth comparing this with another version of the same program which (*mea culpa*) the author wrote before being converted to the concept of a structured approach to programming!

```
10 DIM L(100)
20 GOSUB 190
30 INPUT N
40 L=1
50 H=I-1
60 M=U
70 IF L<=H AND L(M)<> N THEN GOTO 90
80 GOTO 150
90 IF L(M)>N THEN GOTO 120
100 L=M+1
110 GOTO 130
120 H=M-1
130 M=INT((L+H)/2)
140 GOTO 70
150 IF L(M)<> N THEN PRINT "not found"
160 IF L(M)<> N THEN STOP
170 PRINT L(M);"FOUND AT ";M
180 STOP
190 FOR I= 1 TO 100
200 INPUT L(I)
210 IF L(I)=0 THEN RETURN
220 NEXT I
```

This is a good example of what is called 'spaghetti'-type programming and is often the consequence of sitting down at a keyboard and writing the program there and then. It does not really matter if one is not interested in writing programs for other people to understand, but it is, unfortunately, quite difficult to follow the logic of one's own program some time after it was written.

Now we can go back to our original problem of finding the telephone numbers associated with certain names. We will store our 'directory' as a list of strings; each string will represent an entry in the directory and will be made up of two parts. These will be the name followed by the number. The two parts will be separated by a marker, a * character as follows:

SMITH JOHN*01-234-8976

We then have to decide what part of each string is to be used as a 'key' to the record. For this example we will use the first four characters of the name—the "SMIT" part in the above example. Now computers store everything in numerical codes, even the letters of the alphabet, and so they know that, say, "ANNA" comes after "ADAM" and "SMIT" comes before "SMYT". So once we have our list of names and numbers stored in memory we can perform a similar kind of search as with our earlier program:

58

```
1.  ARRAY list$(1:100)
2.  LET index:=1
3.  READ list$(index)
4.  LOOP WHILE list$(index)<>0
5.     LET index=index+1
6.     READ list$(index)
7.  REPEAT
8.  LET length=index-1
9.  READ name$
10.LET key$:=LEFT(name$,4)
11.LET lo:=1
12.LET hi:=length
13.LET mid:=CHOP((lo+hi)/2)
14.LOOP WHILE lo<=hi
15.    LET mid:=CHOP((lo+hi)/2)
16.    IF key$=LEFT(list$(mid),4)
17.       THEN
18.          PRINT list$(mid)
19.       ELSE
20.          IF key$>LEFT(list$(mid),4)
21.             THEN
22.                LET lo:=mid+1
23.             ELSE
24.                LET hi:=mid-1
25.             IFEND
26.    IFEND
27.REPEAT
28.PRINT name$;"not found"
29.END
```

The instruction in pseudo-code lines 16 and 20 contains LEFT(**string$,k**) which is used to extract the **k** left-most characters of **string$**.

Only one thing remains before writing the BASIC program from this and that is to amend line 18. What we should do in order to make the output look more understandable is to present it in the form of:

SMITH JOHN Telephone No 01-234-8976

We can do this by searching along the string until we find the * marker which separates the name from the number. We can approach it as a separate program in which we search a string for the marker and divide it into two parts:

1. Input string$
2. Search string$ for the *.
3. Print all of string$ to the left of the marker.
4. Print all the remainder of string$.

So we have to search for the * and to do this we will go through a loop searching for this symbol and note its position when found. This is very similar to the routine carried out in the vowel-searching program in Example 2.

1. Input string$.
2. Loop for length of string$ character by character.
3.   If the character in string$ is "*"
4.     Then
5.       Print the position of the character in string$.
6.       Print the left-most part of string$ up to "*" position.
7.       Print the right-most part of string$.
8.       Stop.
9.     Else
10.       Do nothing.
11.   Ifend.
12.Repeat.
13.End.

In other words:

```
1.  READ string$
2.  LOOP FOR i=1 TO length
3.    IF string$(i)="*"
4.      THEN
5.        PRINT LEFT(string$(i-1))
6.        PRINT RIGHT(string$(length-i))
7.        STOP
8.      ELSE
9.        SKIP
10.  IFEND
11. REPEAT
12. END
```

This is fine but we ought never to give our computer the chance to make a fool of us. It is always possible that the data in our list might be in error either through from corruption or from an error on the part of the person who typed the data in the first place. In either case we should allow for the possibility that no "*" is found by making our program take this into account:

```
1.  READ string$
2.  LOOP FOR i=1 TO length
3.    IF string$(i)="*"
4.      THEN
5.        PRINT LEFT(string$(i-1))
6.        PRINT "TELEPHONE NO-";RIGHT(string$(length-i))
7.        STOP
8.      ELSE
9.        SKIP
10.  IFEND
11. REPEAT
12. PRINT "DELIMITING CHARACTER NOT FOUND IN RECORD"
13. END
```

If we call this subprogram PHONENO then we can incorporate it into our big program by transferring the string to be printed to it and letting it get on with the job:

**60**

```
1. ARRAY list$(1:100)
2. LET index:=1
3. READ list$(index)
4. LOOP WHILE list$(index)<>0
5.    LET index=index+1
6.    READ list$(index)
7. REPEAT
8. LET length=index-1
9. READ name$
10.LET key$:=LEFT(name$,4)
11.LET lo:=1
12.LET hi:=length
13.LET mid:=CHOP((lo+hi)/2)
14.LOOP WHILE lo<=hi
15.    LET mid:=CHOP((lo+hi)/2)
16.    IF key$=LEFT(list$(mid),4)
17.       THEN
18.          EXECUTE PHONENO(list$(mid))
19.       ELSE
20.          IF key$>LEFT(list$(mid),4)
21.             THEN
22.                LET lo:=mid+1
23.             ELSE
24.                LET hi:=mid-1
25.             IFEND
26.    IFEND
27.REPEAT
28.PRINT name$;"not found"
29.END
```

We will now draw up a new data table:

| Logical Name | Purpose | Type | BASIC variable name |
|---|---|---|---|
| list$ | list of names | string array index (1:100) | L$ |
| index | index to list | integer | INDEX% |
| length | length of list | integer | LENGTH% |
| name$ | name being searched for | string | N$ |
| key$ | first four characters of name | string | K$ |

| lo | index of bottom of sublist | integer | LO% |
|---|---|---|---|
| hi | index of top of sublist | integer | HI% |
| mid | mid-point index of sublist | integer | MID% |

A BASIC program to do this is shown below:

```
10 DIM L$(100)
20 INDEX%=1
30 INPUT L$(INDEX%)
40 WHILE L$(INDEX%)<>"ZZZZ"
50   INDEX%=INDEX%+1
60   INPUT L$(INDEX%)
70 WEND
80 LENGTH%=INDEX%-1
90 INPUT N$
95 K$=LEFT$(N$,4)
100 LO%=1
110 HI%=LENGTH%
120 MID%=INT((LO%+HI%)/2)
130 WHILE LO%<=HI%
140   MID%=INT((LO%+HI%)/2)
150   IF K$=LEFT$(L$(MID%),4) THEN GOTO 190
        ELSE IF K$>LEFT$(L$(MID%),4) THEN LO%=MID%+1 ELSE HI%=MID%-1
160 WEND
170 PRINT N$;"not found"
180 STOP
190 FOR I%=1 TO LEN(L$(MID%))
191 IF MID$(L$(MID%),I%,1)="*" THEN GOTO 1000
192 NEXT I%
193 PRINT"DELIMITER NOT FOUND"
200 STOP
1000 PRINT LEFT$(L$(MID%),I%-1);
1010 PRINT "TELEPHONE NO-";
1020 PRINT RIGHT$(L$(MID%),LEN(L$(MID%))-I%)
1030 END
```

Test this with suitable data and it should work very satisfactorily. However, there are one or two extras which we really ought to consider if we are going to use this program in a practical sense. One of these is that it is quite possible that we might have several telephone numbers in our list which have the same first four characters of the name in common. For example:

JONES J.G*0480-67543
JONES K.R*0780-734116
JONES T.P.E*0890-67543

or even

DAVIDSON T.H.\*0564-657899
DAVIES MARY\*0321-7689
DAVIS R.R.F\*01-564-2314

How should we deal with these ? One way is to find the first name whose first four characters match the key and then print all those names which follow it with the same key. But beware, you may have to go both backwards and forwards from the matching name since it is quite possible for the sublists to split with some names with the same key in both adjacent sublists both above and below the match. Luckily it is not a difficult programming task to build this into a program which has been designed in this way. Do not forget that this method can only be applied to a list which is held in a table in memory. If you want to apply it to a file held on backing store then the only way you can do it is to have a disk file which you can access in a random manner, as with the sorting program shown in Example 7.

Another way of searching for data which are held in some sort of a file is to use what is termed a 'hashing' method. In this case we use the key to each record, a name or a number, to give us the position in the file where we might find the data. For example, we might use the actual part number itself as the key to its location within a large file of parts. Once having obtained the key we can, as it were, 'unlock' all the details of that part. Let us take an example where we have a file, in this case a list held in memory, of account numbers. To simplify matters we will only allow for 100 accounts. The account numbers can have three digits and this means that we can have numbers from 001 to 999. What we do is to effect a transformation of the account number, called 'hashing', so that it is reduced to a number in the range 1 to 100. There are all sorts of ways of doing this and in this case we will:

1. Divide the account number by 100. Take the whole number part of the answer.
2. Multiply the whole number obtained by 100.
3. Subtract the answer obtained from the account number plus one.

This is a routine all on its own which we will call HASH. It requires input of the account number and it will calculate the record number:

```
SUBPROGRAM HASH(accountno,recno)
1. LET result:=CHOP(accountno/100)
2. LET result:=result*100
3. LET recno:=1+accountno-result
END OF SUBPROGRAM
```

Therefore, if we have an account number of 651 the record number where all the details of that account are stored will be 52; (1+651-6*100).

It is not very difficult to see that as well as the account number we would also expect to see the details of the account itself in record 52 as well. It turns out that this is not really a problem, as we shall see if we look at the steps needed to be taken to place the records into the list in places where they can easily be found again. First of all, if we are going to have 100 accounts dealt with in this way, we have to set up an empty list in the following way:

```
1. ARRAY list$(1:100)
2. LOOP FOR index=1 TO 100
3.    LET list$(index):="000"
4. REPEAT
```

This places sets of three zeros in every element of **list** so that when we have calculated a record number the first thing we do is to ensure that the record is empty by looking for "000". Then we can process the details of each account and place them in the appropriate record in the list:

```
5. READ accountno
6. LOOP
7.    READ accountdetails$
8.    LET account$:=accountno
9.    EXECUTE HASH(accountno,recno)
10.   IF list$(recno)<>"000"
11.     THEN
12.        LET recno:=recno+1
13.           IF recno>100
14.             THEN
15.                LET recno:=1
16.             ELSE
17.                SKIP
18.           IFEND
19.     ELSE
20.   IFEND
21.   LET list$(recno):=account$+accountdetails$
22.   READ accountno
23. REPEAT UNTIL accountno=0
```

Our data table would be:

| Logical name | Purpose | Type | BASIC variable name |
|---|---|---|---|
| **list$** | list of accounts and details | string array index (1:100) | L$ |

**64**

| | | | |
|---|---|---|---|
| **index** | index to list$ | integer | INDEX% |
| **accountno** | account number | real | ACCOUNT |
| **recno** | record number | integer | RECNO% |
| **account$** | string conversion of **accountno** | string | N$ |
| **accountdetails$** | data relating to **account$** | string | A$ |
| **result** | temporary storage in HASH sub program | real | RESULT |

Here is a BASIC program written to do this:

```
10 DIM L$(100)
20 FOR I%=1 TO 100
30 L$(I%)="000"
40 NEXT I%
50 INPUT"ACCOUNT NO"; ACCOUNT
60 IF ACCOUNT=0 THEN STOP
70 INPUT "DETAILS";A$
80 N$=STR$(ACCOUNT)
90 GOSUB 120
100 IF L$(RECNO%)<> "000" THEN GOTO 160 ELSE L$(RECNO%)=N$+A$
110 GOTO 50
120 RESULT=INT(ACCOUNT/100)
130 RESULT=RESULT*100
140 RECNO%=1+ACCOUNT-RESULT
150 RETURN
160 RECNO%=RECNO%+1
170 IF RECNO%>100 THEN RECNO%=1
180 GOTO 100
```

Having once set up the data in the table any item in that table can be searched for using the HASH routine again. Once the account number has been input to the program the hash value can be calculated and the details for that account searched for since, if the account details are not held in the record given by HASH, then successive records are searched until the correct account is found.

Once we have a file full of records in locations defined by the key to each of these records — the account number in this example — we can write a program similar to the one we have just written in order to gain access to whichever record we wish. All we need to do is to calculate the hash value of the account number, go to that record, and see if it is the one we want. If it is, then fine. If it is not, then we begin to search through the file in sequence from that record remembering that if we reach the end of the file, the hundredth record in our example, we have to go to record 1 next. The amount of searching is therefore cut down enormously. So we would write:

1. Loop while there are accounts to be processed.
2. Read in the account number to be searched for.
3. Execute the HASH subprogram.
4. Go to the record number given by HASH.
5. If the record at that location is the one required then process that record and ask for next record number for processing.
6. Otherwise go to the next record in sequence.
7. If the next record number exceeds 100 go to record number 1.
8. Repeat until 100 records have been examined.
9. Write a message to say that the record has not been found.
10. Repeat.

Now because our example is based on a list which is held in memory and will be lost if we load and run another program we will place our program at the end of the last one we wrote so that once our list has been set up in memory we can immediately start examining it. The situation would be different if the records of the various accounts were held on a file on backing store. In this case we can read the records into memory and once they have been processed they can be written back onto the file. It will be left to the reader to amend the program to do this. Of course, using a random access file makes the task a lot easier.

```
24.READ accountno
25.LOOP
26.   EXECUTE HASH(accountno,recno)
27.   LET account$:=accountno
28.   LOOP WHILE  LEFT(list$(recno),3)<>account$
29.      LET recno:=recno+1
30.      IF recno>100
31.         THEN
32.            LET recno:=1
33.         ELSE
34.            SKIP
35.      IFEND
36.   REPEAT
37.   EXECUTE PROCESSACC(accountno)
38.READ accountno$
39.REPEAT UNTIL accountno=0
40.END
```

**66**

The PROCESSACC subprogram would be one where accounts would be amended and updated. Whatever goes on inside that subprogram would not affect what happens in the main program. The data table requires no amendment and so the complete BASIC program looks like:

```
10  DIM L$(100)
20  FOR I%=1 TO 100
30  L$(I%)="000"
40  NEXT I%
45  REM**SETTING UP ACCOUNTS***
50  INPUT"ACCOUNT NO"; ACCOUNT
60  IF ACCOUNT=0 THEN GOTO 220
70  INPUT "DETAILS";A$
80  REM*** IN THE VERSION OF BASIC USED TO TEST THIS PROGRAM ***
90  REM*** THE STR$ FUNCTION PLACED A BLANK IN FRONT OF THE FIRST ***
100 REM*** CHARACTER OF N$ MAKING IT FOUR CHARACTERS LONG ***
110 N$=STR$(ACCOUNT)
120 GOSUB 150
130 IF L$(RECNO%)<> "000" THEN GOTO 190 ELSE L$(RECNO%)=N$+A$
140 GOTO 50
150 RESULT=INT(ACCOUNT/100)
160 RESULT=RESULT*100
170 RECNO%=1+ACCOUNT-RESULT
180 RETURN
190 RECNO%=RECNO%+1
200 IF RECNO%>100 THEN RECNO%=1
210 GOTO 130
215 REM**SEARCHING FOR ACCOUNTS**
220 INPUT "ACCOUNT NO";ACCOUNT
230 IF ACCOUNT=0 THEN STOP
240 GOSUB 150
250 N$=STR$(ACCOUNT)
260 REM*** SEE REM ON LINES 80,90,100 ***
270 IF LEFT$(L$(RECNO%),4)<>N$ THEN GOTO 280 ELSE GOTO 320
280 RECNO%=RECNO%+1
290 PRINT RECNO%-1
300 IF RECNO%>100 THEN RECNO%=1
310 GOTO 270
320 PRINT "ACCOUNT NO: ";L$(RECNO%);" FOUND"
330 REM*** THIS IS WHERE THE ACCOUNT DETAILS CAN BE AMENDED ***
340 REM*** AND THEY CAN BE REPLACED IN THE RECORD ***
350 GOTO 220
```

You will notice that there is no provision for the situation where the account number you input is not found. That is another extra section you should be able to insert in the program yourself.

The hash coding program just dealt with is an example of a program which does two things in the one program: it sets up the records in places where they can easily be found and it allows us to find those records easily and quickly. This next section is really aimed at the people who have a disk drive on their computer and although it cannot be used if you have a tape drive it might spur on those who wonder just whether disks are really useful. The point is that disks are useful not only for storing data but also for storing programs. You probably knew that but have you considered the possibility of getting programs to load other programs? It is a technique known as 'chaining' and is of great use if you have the kind of situation where you have a number of related programs, such as the two above, and you might want to choose to use only one of them. For example, if you already have your accounts set up you may only want to perform regular amendments on them. You may not want the overhead of memory to be taken up by programs you do not want to use. So if we only use the programs we want at any time then the whole system is going to be much more efficient. If you have a program which provides you with a 'menu' of options then only the program you actually want to use is in memory. This means that you can write programs to perform specific tasks and use them as they are wanted without embedding them in much longer programs. This is an encouragement to write shorter programs and also enables programming to become a group activity where each member of the group writes one small program; these small programs will then require one main program to pull them all together.

A 'menu' could look like this:

### SCHOOL BANK

Do you want to set up the accounts?.................................... (1)
Do you want to amend accounts?...................................... (2)
Do you want to print out details of all accounts?.............. (3)
Finish?................................................................................ (4)
Type 1,2,3, or 4

What you are asking the user to do is to select one of four options; do not forget option 4 otherwise you have put them in a situation from which they cannot escape. We can write an outline of what we want to do like this:

1. SELECT **number** FROM 4 CASES
2. CASE 1
3.   CHAIN SETUP
4. CASE 2
5.   CHAIN AMEND
6. CASE 3
7.   CHAIN PRINTOUT
8. CASE 4
9.   STOP
10.DEFAULT
11.  PRINT"Only the numbers 1,2,3, or 4 are acceptable"
12.SELECTEND

CHAIN means 'Load and run the named program'. We have

already written the SETUP program and part of the AMEND program, although they have had to be combined in our last example. The PRINTOUT program has not been written yet, but that does not stop us from referring to it. It can be written separately later on. The MENU program which allows us to chain would look like this in BASIC:

```
10 PRINT"                    SCHOOL BANK"
20 PRINT
30 PRINT"Do you want to set up the accounts ?.................(1)"
40 PRINT
50 PRINT"Do you want to amend accounts ?.....................(2)"
60 PRINT
70 PRINT"Do you want to print out details of all accounts ?..(3)"
80 PRINT
90 PRINT"Finish ?............................................(4)"
100 PRINT
110 PRINT"                    Type 1,2,3 or 4"
120 INPUT NUMBER
130 ON NUMBER GOTO 140,150,160,170,180
140 CHAIN"SETUP"
150 CHAIN"AMEND"
160 CHAIN"PRINTOUT"
170 STOP
180 PRINT"Only the numbers 1,2,3 and 4 are acceptable"
190 GOTO 110
```

## Then we can write the SETUP program as:

```
10 DIM L$(100)
20 FOR I%=1 TO 100
30 L$(I%)="000"
40 NEXT I%
50 INPUT"ACCOUNT NO"; ACCOUNT
60 IF ACCOUNT=0 THEN CHAIN "MENU"
70 INPUT "DETAILS";A$
80 N$=STR$(ACCOUNT)
90 GOSUB 120
100 IF L$(RECNO%)<> "000" THEN GOTO 160 ELSE L$(RECNO%)=N$+A$
110 GOTO 50
120 RESULT=INT(ACCOUNT/100)
130 RESULT=RESULT*100
140 RECNO%=1+ACCOUNT-RESULT
150 RETURN
160 RECNO%=RECNO%+1
170 IF RECNO%>100 THEN RECNO%=1
180 GOTO 100
```

Notice that line 60 uses the CHAIN command again to take us back to the menu so that we can exit from the whole thing in an elegant manner. Similarly, the AMEND program can be written as:

```
10 INPUT "ACCOUNT NO";ACCOUNT
20 IF ACCOUNT=0 THEN CHAIN"MENU"
30 GOSUB 140
40 N$=STR$(ACCOUNT)
50 IF LEFT$(L$(RECNO%),4)<>N$ THEN GOTO 60 ELSE GOTO 100
60 RECNO%=RECNO%+1
70 PRINT RECNO%-1
80 IF RECNO%>100 THEN RECNO%=1
90 GOTO 50
100 PRINT "ACCOUNT NO: ";L$(RECNO%);" FOUND"
```

```
110 REM*** THIS IS WHERE THE ACCOUNT DETAILS CAN BE AMENDED ***
120 REM*** AND THEY CAN BE REPLACED IN THE RECORD ***
130 GOTO 10
140 RESULT=INT(ACCOUNT/100)
150 RESULT=RESULT*100
160 RECNO%=1+ACCOUNT-RESULT
170 RETURN
```

See how it has become much neater and easier to understand. There is, however, one problem to overcome. That is the problem of making sure that the AMEND program knows about the list of accounts. As it stands we are going to ask the program to look for an item in a list called L$ in line 50, and that is the first time in this program that L$ has been mentioned. The easiest way to deal with this problem is to store the list on a serial file, which can be on tape anyway, and then to make the first sequence of the program the loading of that file into the list L$ in memory. Then the rest of the program can be run. At the end, before going back to the menu, the amended file can be written back onto the tape file. After all, we would want to keep a permanent copy of the up-to-date file for future processing. Because of the way these programs have been written it becomes very easy to 'splice' these amendments into the programs. In fact, if one were in the position of having no disks and no likelihood of getting them then the whole set of programs would have to be held in memory at one time with a menu at the front which takes the user to the required parts of the program. This in no way precludes the writing of the program in the modular form suggested earlier but it does require a lot of memory for program storage, leaving a restricted amount for the lists which are being manipulated.

# 4 INTRODUCTION TO THE PROJECTS

This chapter leads in to the various suggestions for project work which make up the second part of this book. Many of the projects deal with the uses to which files of data can be put. If you do not have a computer with a disk drive it does not mean that you cannot produce good, useful, and working programs which do all the things covered in the project suggestions. They can all be done, using the programming techniques described, for any microcomputer with a cassette tape player. It just means that you might have to use a certain amount of ingenuity to make the programs efficient and easy to use. But then you will have learned some very useful computing techniques in the process.

In many programs we wish to store a date in a file. We want it to take up as little space as possible and at the same time we want to have it stored so that we can make use of it in some way. For example, we may want to find which of two dates is the later or perhaps to sort the file into date order. If we store the date just as we would speak it—'12th of May', for example—both of these things would be quite difficult to do. A far easier way would be either to store the date simply as the day number of the year so that 1 January is day 1 and 31 December is day 365 or to store the date simply as a number in the form of YYMMDD (821210 for 10 December 1982). For the purpose of this example we shall use the former method. What we have to do is to write a subprogram which will be given the date in the form DD/MM. This means that there are two digits for the day of the month and two digits for the month of the year. There are certain applications where the year is either not necessary or can be assumed to be the current year. The subprogram then returns the day of the year to the main program.

The first thing we have to do is to take account of the different lengths of the months; we will assume that February has 28 days this year. Then we extract the day of the month from the date string and then the month number. We then add up the number of days in the complete months up to the month in question and then add on the days so far of the current month. This gives us the number of days so far after 1 January. In pseudo-code we can write this as:

```
SUBPROGRAM DAYOUT(date$,dayno)
1.  ARRAY days(1:12)
2.  LOOP for index=1 to 12
3.    LET days(index):=31,28,31,30,31,30,31,31,30,31,30,31
4.  REPEAT
5.  LET day:=LEFT(date$,2)
6.  LET month:=RIGHT(date$,2)
7.  LET dayno:=0
8.  IF month=1
9.    THEN
10.     LET dayno:=day
11.     RETURN TO MAIN PROGRAM
12.   ELSE
13.     LOOP for index=1 to month-1
14.       LET dayno:=dayno+days(index)
15.     REPEAT
16. IFEND
17. LET dayno:=dayno+day
END OF SUBPROGRAM
```

Line 3 of the above program is the author's shorthand way of saying that **days**(1) will contain 31, **days**(2) will contain 28, and so on.

Our next move is to set up the data table prior to writing the program in BASIC:

| Logical name | Purpose | Type | BASIC variable name |
|---|---|---|---|
| **days** | list of days of months | numeric array index (1:12) | D |
| **index** | index to **days** | integer | I% |
| **date$** | date in DD/MM format | string | D$ |
| **day** | day number extracted from **date$** | real | D |
| **month** | month number extracted from **date$** | real | M |

**72**

| | | | |
|---|---|---|---|
| **dayno** | number of days from Jan. 1st | real | N |

The BASIC program can be written as:

```
10 REM***THIS SUBROUTINE REQUIRES TO BE GIVEN THE DATE***
20 REM***IN THE FORM DD/MM VIA THE VARIABLE***
30 REM***D$. IT RETURNS THE DAY OF THE YEAR NUMBER IN N***
40 DIM D(12)
50 FOR I%=1 TO 12
60 READ D(I%)
70 NEXT I%
80 D=VAL(LEFT$(D$,2))
90 M=VAL(RIGHT$(D$,2))
100 N=0
110 IF M=1 THEN GOTO 150
120 FOR I%=1 TO M-1
130 N=N+D(I%)
140 NEXT I%
150 N=N+D
160 DATA 31,28,31,30,31,30,31,31,30,31,30,31
```

In order to proceed in the other direction to convert the day-of-the-year number into a proper date we need another subprogram called DAYIN which in pseudo-code will look like this:

```
SUBPROGRAM DAYIN(dayno,date$)
1.  ARRAY days(1:12)
2.  ARRAY names$(1:12)
3.  LOOP for index=1 to 12
4.     LET days(index):=31,28,31,30,31,30,31,31,30,31,30,31
5.     LET names$(index):=JAN,FEB,MAR,APR,MAY,JUN,JUL,AUG,SEP,OCT,NOV,DEC
6.  REPEAT
7.  LOOP for index=1 to 12
8.     LET dayno:=dayno+days(index)
9.     IF dayno<=0
10.       THEN
11.          LET dayno:=dayno-days(index)
12.          LET date$:=dayno$+names$(index)+"83"
13.          RETURN TO MAIN PROGRAM
14.       ELSE
15.          SKIP
16.    IFEND
17. REPEAT
END OF SUBPROGRAM
```

The data table for this will be:

| Logical name | Purpose | Type | BASIC variable name |
|---|---|---|---|
| **days** | list of days of months | numeric array index (1:12) | D |

| names$ | list of names of months | string array index (1:12) | M$ |
|---|---|---|---|
| index | index to **days** and **names$** | integer | I% |
| date$ | date in DD month$ 83 format | string | D$ |
| month | month number extracted from **date$** | real | M |
| dayno | number of days from Jan. 1st | real | N |
| dayno$ | **dayno** in string form | string | N$ |

Written in BASIC this becomes:

```
10 REM***THIS SUBROUTINE REQUIRES THE DAY NUMBER,N***
20 REM***AND WILL RETURN THE STRING D$ CONTAINING THE***
30 REM***DAY,MONTH & YEAR***
40 DIM D(12)
50 DIM M$(12)
60 FOR I%=1 TO 12
70 READ D(I%)
80 NEXT I%
90 FOR I%=1 TO 12
100 READ M$(I%)
110 NEXT I%
120 FOR I%=1 TO 12
130 N=N-D(I%)
140 IF N<=0 THEN GOTO 170
150 NEXT I%
160 STOP
170 N=N+D(I%)
180 N$=STR$(N)
190 D$=N$+" "+M$(I%)+" 83"
200 DATA 31,28,31,30,31,30,31,31,30,31,30,31
210 DATA JAN,FEB,MAR,APR,MAY,JUN,JUL,AUG,SEP,OCT,NOV,DEC
```

The next thing to do before moving on to some practical problems is to look at the way we store data in each record of a file. For the purpose of this we are going to use the term **file** for either a set of records stored in memory in a list or a set of records stored on tape or disk. Whether we are referring to files held on disk, tape, or as a list in memory the techniques are all basically the same. First, we have to realize that on the vast majority of microcomputers we store data in character format. In other words, we store strings of characters in the file.This means that we can store names and numbers but the numbers are stored as the set of characters which make them up and not as the numbers themselves. This means that any numbers stored on a file have to be converted from a string of characters into numerical form before any arithmetic can be performed. We use the BASIC VAL instruction to do the conversion when numbers are read from a file and the STR$ instruction before writing the numbers to the file. You can perhaps now see why we can keep files in memory in the form of lists of character strings and treat them in the same way as random access files held on a magnetic disc. The disadvantage of storing the files in memory is that very few microcomputers have sufficient RAM (Random Access Memory) available for the storage of very large files. Nevertheless, even with restricted file space available the principles of handling files of real live data can be demonstrated—as in Example 5.

Each record in a file can either be **fixed length** or **variable length**. A fixed length record, as its name implies, is one where only a certain number of characters are available for the storage of the data in that record and the record is divided up into a number of clearly defined **fields**. For example, each record of a file may contain a part number, description, cost price, selling price, and number in stock. The space within the record could be allocated so that 6 characters are reserved for the part number, 20 for the description, 5 for the cost price, 6 for the selling price and 5 for the number in stock. This means that the record is split up into a series of fields or 'slots' into which the data are placed:

```
. . . . . ! . . . . . . . . . . . . . . . . . . . . ! . . . . ! . . . . . . ! . . . .
no.    description        cost  selling no.in
                          price price   stock
```

Thus the record for an item numbered 453317,a transistor radio, with a cost price of £21.35, selling at £33.95, with 325 in stock would look like this:

453317TRANSISTOR RADIO     21.35 33.95 325

Notice that the record is 42 characters long and the name starts at character 7 and is allowed to be no more than 20 characters long, as it must not spill over into the field which starts at the twenty-seventh character which is the cost price. Characters 32 to 37 contain the selling price and the last five characters (38 to 42) store the number actually in stock. We can write a short subprogram called READOUT which will collect the details we want from any specified record in the file, wherever it is stored. We could write this as:

```
SUBPROGRAM READOUT(datastring$,partno,description$,cost,
                   sellingprice,stock)
1. LET partno:=LEFT(datastring$,6)
2. LET description$:=datastring$(7,26)
3. LET cost:=datastring$(27,31)
4. LET sellingprice:=datastring$(32,37)
5. LET stock:=RIGHT(datastring$,5)
END OF SUBPROGRAM
```

The two numbers in brackets are used to indicate the start and finish of the part of the string we wish to extract, so that **datastring$** (32,37) means 'that part of the datastring from character 32 to character 37'—very easy really!

Note that the subprogram is used to return the values of the variables **partno**, **description$**, **cost**, **sellingprice**, **stock** having been given **datastring$** which contains the record.

A subprogram to place the data into the record could be called READIN and in it the various pieces of data can be placed into the appropriate parts of a blank **datastring$** so that a complete record is assembled prior to being inserted in its proper place in the file.

On the other hand, a record will be of variable length when we are unable to assign an exact number of characters to the data it contains. This is because we may not be in a position to say that every record in the file is going to be of the same length. This could happen in a file which holds records of transactions within a bank account. Each account can hold a maximum number of transactions, limited by the maximum number of characters which can be held in a single string—usually 255. If we say that after the account number, say five digits, we will have 250 characters left in each record of a file then we can begin by saying that each transaction on an account will be either a paying-in or a withdrawal, on a particular date and for a particular amount. If each transaction is denoted by a code letter, this leaves the opportunity open for different types of transactions, if necessary, the date can be coded into three digits by DAYOUT, and the amount of the transaction needs a maximum of, say, seven digits. The seven digits for the amount are for a decimal point, although this can be avoided if space is tight, four digits for the pounds and two for the pence. This means that amounts from 0000.01 up to 9999.99 can be recorded. All this means that each transaction needs 11 characters, thus allowing up to 22 transactions to be stored in one record. The spare characters could be used for storing other information about the account holder if necessary. Each record in the file will then consist of the account number— five characters—and a series of groups of 11 characters each storing details of one transaction. So the record for account number 10235 could look like this:

10235I0770034.7800910056.66I1020100.00I1050245.30/

telling us that on day 77—18 March—£34.78 was paid in, on day 91—1 April—£56.66 was taken out, on day 102—12 April—£100.00 was paid in, and on day 105—15 April—£245.30 was paid in. The / character defines the end of the record.

Each record can be decoded in 'packets' of data each 11 characters long which can be themselves decoded in the following way:

```
SUBPROGRAM DECODE(transaction$,transactioncode$,
                  date$,amount)
1. LET transactioncode$:=LEFT(transaction$,1)
2. LET dayno:=transactioncode$(2,4)
3. EXECUTE DAYIN(dayno,date$)
4. LET amount:=RIGHT(transaction$,7)
END OF SUBPROGRAM
```

To read and decode the data on the file we can write:

```
SUBPROGRAM READDATA(recordno)
1.  READ record$ from record number recordno
2.  LET accountno$:=LEFT(record$,5)
3.  LOOP for counter=0 to 21
4.      LET transaction$:=record$(6+counter*11,16+counter*11)
5.      IF LEFT(transaction$,1)="/"
6.          THEN
7.              RETURN TO MAIN PROGRAM
8.          ELSE
9.              EXECUTE DECODE(transaction$,transactioncode$,
                  date$,amount)
10.             PROCESS THE DATA READ FROM THE FILE
11.     IFEND
12. REPEAT
END OF SUBPROGRAM
```

To add an extra transaction to an account record all we have to do is to code the date of the transaction and its type and then place these data together with the amount involved after the last transaction for the account. This will involve finding the end of the record string and placing the new transaction details on the record and placing a new "/" character after the new transaction details. If we call the routine to do this ADDTRANS we can write this as:

```
SUBPROGRAM ADDTRANS(recordno)
1.  READ date$
2.  READ transactiontype$
3.  LOOP
4.     IF transactiontype$<>"DEBIT" OR "CREDIT"
5.        THEN
6.           PRINT"WRONG TRANSACTION TYPE - RE-INPUT"
7.        ELSE
8.           SKIP
9.     IFEND
10.    READ transactiontype$
11. REPEAT UNTIL transactiontype$="DEBIT" OR "CREDIT"
12. IF transactiontype$="CREDIT"
13.    THEN
14.       LET type$:="I"
15.    ELSE
16.       LET type$:="O"
17. IFEND
18. READ amount
19. IF lengthamount<7
20.    THEN
21.       LOOP
22.          LET amount$:="0"+amount$
23.       REPEAT UNTIL lengthamount=7
24.    ELSE
25.       SKIP
26. IFEND
27. EXECUTE DAYOUT(date$,dayno)
28. IF lengthday<3
29.    THEN
30.       LOOP
31.          LET dayno$:="0"+dayno$
32.       REPEAT UNTIL lengthday=3
33.    ELSE
34.       SKIP
35. IFEND
36. LET data$:=dayno$+type$+amount$+"/"
37. READ record$ from record number recordno
38. LET newdata$:=LEFT(record$,(lengthrecord-1))+data$
39. WRITE newdata$ back to record number recordno
END OF SUBPROGRAM
```

The parts of the program in lines 18 to 25 and 27 to 34 ensure that the amount and the day number contain the correct number of characters. They are packed out with zeros at the start to make them the correct length.

Note that we use the variables **lengthamount** to store the number of characters in **amount**, **dayno$** to be the string equivalent of **dayno**, and **lengthrecord** to store the number of characters in **record$**; **lengthday** is the number of characters in the string equivalent, **dayno$**, of **dayno**. It should also be noted that there are no checks built in which test to see if the date is valid. What if 31/02/83 is input?

Something else should be considered before adding further fields into a variable length record. It is always possible that there are already 22 transactions stored in the record. What should we do then ? Probably the easiest thing to do is to dump the complete record into another, overspill, record at the end of the file, and start off from new again with the existing record. We could then use some of the unused spare characters at the end of the record to give the number of the record where the previous transactions are stored. When we come to print the entire collection of transactions for one account we would look after the / character to see if there were any sets of transactions to be printed out before those in the current record. Then we would know where to find them. They could then be printed out before the contents of the current record and so produce a set of account records which contained more than 22 transactions.

At this point we ought to consider two problems involved in printing out the bank account in the proper format. Remember that the usual form is:

| Date | Debits | Credits | Balance |
| --- | --- | --- | --- |

so that when we set about printing the statement for each of the accounts we have to extract the information relating to each transaction, decode the date, decide whether it is a debit (paying out) or credit (paying in), and then adjust the balance accordingly and print the debit or credit under the correct heading. We should also remember that the first entry in the list of transactions for that account is treated as what is called the 'opening balance' and is the starting point for the running total of the balance. In other words it is that amount to which everything else is added to or subtracted from. So here we can write a subprogram called PRINTBAL. As written here it only takes account of the transactions which are stored in one record of the file. If there is a spill-over into another record because more than 22 transactions have taken place a neat little exercise is provided for the reader to program.

Just before we write PRINTBAL we need to fill in the details contained in line 10 of the subprogram called READDATA where we will calculate the current balance and print the line for that transaction on the statement. We will need to know the type of transaction, the date, and the amount of the transaction together with the balance so far. So let us expand line 10 as follows:

```
10a. IF counter=0
10b.    THEN
```

```
10c.    LET balance:=0
10d.  ELSE
10e.     SKIP
10f. IFEND
10g. IF transactioncode$="I"
10h.   THEN
10i.    LET balance:=balance+amount
10j.  ELSE
10k.    LET balance:=balance-amount
10l. IFEND
10m. EXECUTE PRINTBAL(transactioncode$,date$,amount,balance)
```

The subprogram PRINTBAL decides how the printing is to be set out on the page as follows:

```
SUBPROGRAM PRINTBAL(transactioncode$,date$,amount,balance)
1.  IF amount=balance
2.    THEN
3.       PRINT date$,"Opening balance",SPACES,balance
4.    ELSE
5.      IF transactioncode$="I"
6.         THEN
7.            PRINT date$,SPACES,amount,balance
8.         ELSE
9.            PRINT date$,amount,SPACES,balance
10.     IFEND
11. IFEND
END OF SUBPROGRAM
```

SPACES indicates that a number of spaces must be left before printing the next number. How many spaces is decided by the size of display being used. The PRINTBAL subprogram would allow you to make use of any formatting statements you might have available in the language you are using—PRINT USING, for example, in BASIC. Look at PRINTBAL very carefully. There could be a problem on certain occasions when it is used. It is left up to you to spot this problem and decide on a way around it.

# 5 PROJECTS

## Project 1—An indexing problem

The first project involves the computerization of what is a very necessary but tedious task—after all, that is why we use computers in the first place. The problem of producing an index to, say, a catalogue or a textbook falls into three parts. The first of these is the transcription of the items in the catalogue and their page references into a list. These will usually be in order of page numbers as the indexer progresses through the book. Alphabetically, of course, the references will be in no order at all and the second task of the program is to sort these into alphabetical order. After this task is complete the last problem is to take redundant references out and replace them with composite references so that

Jelly, calves foot............................................................12
Jelly, calves foot............................................................51
Jelly, calves foot............................................................66

becomes

Jelly, calves foot..................................................12/51/66

This involves editing the list of entries once they have all been entered and sorted. The entry of the items as the contents of each page in the book or catalogue is dealt with can rarely be accomplished in one session and so the program has to be written in such a way that new entries are appended to the list. This means that the program must keep a record of the position in the list of each entry. In our example we will assume that the list is held in memory having previously been stored on either disk or tape. There are variations on the method but the general principles are common to all treatments. Each entry in the list will consist of a reference and a page number which will be

stored with a delimiting character between them, such as a /
character. For example:

ICI Sheep dip/9

however, do not forget that the entry, if it is to serve as a really
useful index, should also be stored as

Sheep dip ICI/9

as well. To be really thorough one should take care to have all
possible combinations of the entry in the index.

The top-down design for the entry of all the items into the
index list is quite simple and will be:

1. Start at the next available blank record in the list.
2. Loop while there are records to be added to the list.
3. Input the reference and its page number.
4. Repeat.

This becomes the following in pseudo-code:

```
1.  ARRAY list$(1:1000)
2.  PRINT "Starting record number"
3.  READ index
4.  PRINT "Reference"
5.  READ reference$
6.  LOOP WHILE reference$<>"END"
7.     PRINT "Page No."
8.     READ page$
9.     LET list$(index):=reference$+"/"+page$
10.    LET index:=index+1
11.    PRINT "Reference"
12.    READ reference$
13. REPEAT
14. PRINT "Last record entered was No.",index-1
```

When all the entries which will make up the index have been
placed into the list, in all their forms, any one of the sorting
methods previously described can be used to produce the
alphabetical listing. The sorting must be done on the reference
alone and so this and the page number must be decoded from
each entry in the list.

A simple routine to decode the data would be:

1. Read through each record character by character
   accumulating the characters read into a variable called **key$**
   until the "/" is reached.
2. Allocate the remainder of the record to the variable called
   **page$**.

```
SUBPROGRAM DECODE(record$,key$,page$)
1. LET key$:=""
2. LET index:=1
3. LOOP
4.    LET key$:=key$+record$(index,1)
5.    LET index:=index+1
6. REPEAT UNTIL record$(index,1)="/"
7. LET page$:=RIGHT(record$,length-index)
END OF SUBPROGRAM
```

The fact that the keys will all be of different lengths does not normally matter. In fact the following is an extract from the index to a catalogue which was produced using this method:

Raddle powder ............................................................... 14
Ranizole paste ............................................................... 11
Ranizole superstrong suspension ............................... 11
Richey spray line aerosol ............................................ 14
Rumbul sheep gun ....................................................... 14
Rumbul sheep pellets .................................................. 14

Remember, however, that when sorting the computer will be told to compare characters and so will treat capital letters differently from lower case letters. This means that we will get:

PARACITICIDE(ANIMALS) ....................................... 11
PIG & POULTRY PRODUCTS ................................... 9
Petroleum jelly ............................................................ 13
Powdered glucose ........................................................ 13
etc.

Once the 'raw' sorted list has been produced the next job is to have a look at it by printing it out. This is easy to do but it is worth doing it properly by making sure that the set of entries which start with the letter "A" are separated from those which start with the letter "B", and so on:

Foster lamb aerosol .................................................... 13
Fox oils ......................................................................... 13

Green oil(carbolized) .................................................. 13

Helmatac in-feed wormer ........................................... 10
Helmatac wormer pellets ........................................... 11
Helmatac ...................................................................... 12

This can be done in the following way:

1. Request number of records to be printed.
2. Set a check key to "A".
3. Loop for the number of records requested.
4. Decode each record into reference and page number.
5. If the check key is not equal to the key
6. Then print a blank line.
7. Replace the check key by the first character of the key just read.
8. Else print the reference followed by enough dots to make a total of 34 characters printed including the page number. Print the page number.
9. Repeat.

```
1.  ARRAY list$(1:1000)
2.  LET key1$:="A"
3.  PRINT"How many records to be printed ?"
4.  READ number
5.  LOOP FOR index= 1 to number
6.     LET record$:=list$(index)
7.     EXECUTE DECODE(record$,key$,page$)
8.     IF key1$<>LEFT(key$,1)
9.        THEN
10.          PRINT SPACES
11.          LET key1$:=LEFT(key$)
12.       ELSE
13.          PRINT "Record no",number,key$
14.          LOOP FOR count=1 TO 34-lengthkey-lengthpage
15.             PRINT "."
16.          REPEAT
17.          PRINT page$
18.    IFEND
19.REPEAT
```

Once the index has been printed it can be examined for repetitions and for redundant entries. This can be done by going to the appropriate entry—you will know its number from the previous printing program—and amending the contents of **page$**. This means that if a series of entries are:

Record no.47 Castor oil .............................................. 23
Record no.48 Castor oil .............................................. 45
Record no.49 Castor oil .............................................. 67

then record number 47 needs to become

Castor oil ........................................................ 23/45/67

and the records numbered 48 and 49 will have to be deleted. First of all we replace each of them with a blank entry. A design to do this would be:

1. Input the record number in the list to be amended.

2. Decode the record.
3. Input the amended page entry.
4. Set up a new record consisting of the old reference followed by the new page entry.
5. Replace the old record by the new record.
6. Place blanks in all the records which have become redundant.

In pseudo-code this becomes:

```
1.  ARRAY list$(1:1000)
2.  PRINT "Record to be amended"
3.  READ number
4.  LOOP WHILE number<>0
5.    LET record$:=list$(number)
6.    EXECUTE DECODE(record$,key$,page$)
7.    PRINT "New pages"
8.    READ page$
9.    LET list$(number):=key$,"/",page$
10.   PRINT "Records to be deleted"
11.   PRINT "First"
12.   READ first
13.   PRINT "Last"
14.   READ last
15.   LOOP FOR index=first TO last
16.     LET list$(index)=""
17.   REPEAT
18.   PRINT "Next number"
19.   READ number
20.REPEAT
```

When the editing is done we have to get rid of the 'holes' in the list. These are the redundant entries which have been replaced by blanks. This is quite easy to do using the following method:

1. Read through the list record by record.
2. Copy each non-blank record into a new list, counting the number of records in the new list.
3. Delete the old list and rename the new list with the name of the old list.

If you cannot carry out the operation in stage 3 simply copy the new list back into the old list thus making it shorter than it was before.

```
SUBPROGRAM SQUASH(array,length)
1.  ARRAY b(1:100)
2.  LET count:=1
3.  LOOP FOR index=1 to length
4.    IF array(count)=0
5.      THEN
6.        SKIP
7.      ELSE
8.        LET b(count):=array(index)
9.        LET count:=count+1
10.   IFEND
11.REPEAT
```

```
12.LET lengthb:=count-1
13.LOOP FOR count=1 to lengthb
14.   LET array(count):=b(count)
15.REPEAT
16.LET length:=lengthb
END OF SUBPROGRAM
```

SQUASH is a good example of what is called a 'housekeeping' routine.

All that has to be done now is to print the index without the record numbers (see line 9 of the printing program) and your indexing is complete. If you want to extend your index for any reason new entries can be added onto the end of the list. Then the list can be sorted again, edited, and printed in its new form.

## Project 2—A simple school bank

The framework for this project has already been sketched out in the previous section but let us pull it all together by defining exactly what we want this series of programs to do. Obviously we need to be able to have a series of programs which carry out a number of defined tasks. In our example these are that there are to be a number of accounts which are to be looked after. Money is paid into these accounts and taken from them in a random manner. In other words, the accounts are not dealt with in order of their number. New accounts have to be added to the system and as people leave the school accounts are withdrawn from the system and closed. At regular intervals statements of the amount of money in all the accounts have to be printed out and distributed to the account holders. A few minutes' reflection will show that the suggestion made earlier will not be completely satisfactory. It is not flexible enough; the one thing about computer programs is that they should be made flexible enough for anyone without detailed computer knowledge to use. So we have to be able to set up a new account, which includes starting up with no accounts on the books, close an account, enter a transaction into an account, and print out a statement of all the accounts or a single selected account. It is also essential for the total of all the money held by the bank at any one time to be available. We will do this by always keeping the grand total in a special account which is amended after each transaction has taken place. Let us write our outline of the selection of the particular program from a menu as follows:

1. SELECT **number** FROM 5 CASES
2. CASE 1

```
3.    CHAIN SETUP
4.  CASE 2
5.    CHAIN CLOSE
6.  CASE 3
7.    CHAIN AMEND
8.  CASE 4
9.    CHAIN PRINTOUT
10.CASE 5
11.  STOP
12.DEFAULT
13.  PRINT "Only the numbers 1,2,3,4 or 5 are acceptable"
14.SELECTEND
```

In all the projects which follow we will refer to records in a file but it will be left to the reader to decide what type of file is to be used depending on the facilities available on the computer system to be used. A system with a disk drive will be able to hold large files which can be manipulated on the disk. On the other hand, if only a cassette tape drive is available all the files will have to be serial files which are read into memory before they can be manipulated, as in one of the earlier examples.

When we get to the SETUP program we must devise a method of allocating an account number, asking for an initial payment in to start the account off, and then writing that information, which is the opening balance, to the record set up in the file to take the information. Then we must ask if there is another account to be set up—we might possibly be in the throes of starting the bank off from scratch—and when no more accounts need to be set up we can return to the main menu.

The CLOSE program will need to print out the balance held in the account and on the payment of that money delete the record from the file and release that account number for future use, otherwise the account numbers will soon run out.

The AMEND program will have to arrange for a record of the amount withdrawn or put into the account to be recorded so that the account is kept up to date.

The PRINTOUT program must allow for either the printing of the details of the transactions up to that date for all the accounts held or simply the details of any one account. One special account number is for the record of the grand total of cash held at any time by the bank.

We have already written a number of subprograms which can be used in this system. They are, to remind you, HASH, DAYOUT, DAYIN, DECODE, READDATA, ADDTRANS, and

PRINTBAL.

The SETUP program would use HASH to allocate the record numbers for each account. Although in the examples given previously we have allowed up to five digits for the account number this could be reduced to three or even two depending on the likely number of accounts. As a rough guide one can say that the number of records available should be about half as big again as the highest account number in order to allow for possible expansion. This means that the number of records allowed for in HASH must be decided upon before the system is set up. The SETUP program should ask for the opening balance, and this is written as the first transaction information after the account number in the record chosen by HASH. Then the amount paid in as an opening balance should be added to the balance kept in the account (suggested number 00000) in order to keep track of the total amount of money in the bank's keeping. So before we use the ADDTRANS subprogram we ought to amend it so that one record in the file, called record 00000, holds the total amount of money held in all the separate accounts. We can do this by placing three more statements at the end of the subprogram :

```
39. READ record$ FROM record (00000)
40. LET record$:=record$+amount$
41. WRITE record$ TO record (00000)
```

## Then SETUP should look rather like this:

```
PROGRAM SETUP
1. READ accountno
2. LOOP
3.     EXECUTE HASH(accountno,,recordno)
4.     READ openingbalance
5.     WRITE accountno$,"I",openingbalance$,"/", TO record(recordno)
6.     READ accountno
7. REPEAT UNTIL accountno=-1
RETURN TO MAIN MENU
```

## Then CLOSE could be:

```
PROGRAM CLOSE
1. READ accountno
2. LOOP
3.     EXECUTE HASH(accoutnno,recordno)
4.     EXECUTE READDATA(recordno)
5.     READ amounttoclose
6.     READ record$ FROM record(00000)
7.     LET record$:=record$-amounttoclose$
8.     WRITE record$ TO record(00000)
9.     LET amount$:="0"
10.    WRITE amount$ TO record(recordno)
11.    READ accountno
12.REPEAT UNTIL accountno=-1
RETURN TO MAIN MENU
```

**88**

## We can write AMEND as:

```
PROGRAM AMEND
1. READ accountno
2. LOOP
3.    EXECUTE HASH(accountno,recordno)
4.    EXECUTE ADDTRANS(recordno)
5.    READ accountno
6. REPEAT UNTIL accountno=-1
RETURN TO MAIN MENU
```

## Finally, PRINTOUT could look like this:

```
PROGRAM PRINTOUT
1. PRINT "All accounts ?"
2. READ response$
3. IF response$="YES"
4.    THEN
5.       LOOP FOR accountno=1 to 99999
6.          EXECUTE HASH(accountno,recordno)
7.          EXECUTE READDATA(recordno)
8.       REPEAT
9.    ELSE
10.   PRINT "Account number ?"
11.   READ accountno
12.      LOOP
13.         EXECUTE HASH(accountno,recordno)
14.         EXECUTE READDATA(recordno)
15.         PRINT "Account number ?"
16.         READ accountno
17.      REPEAT UNTIL accountno=-1
18. IFEND
RETURN TO MAIN MENU
```

# Project 3—A mailing list

We are all familiar with mailing lists; most of us end up on several, often against our will. Creation and maintenance of a mailing list involve a number of separate operations. First of all we have to create the mailing list which will contain names, addresses, possibly telephone numbers, and some code number which may indicate what category of person it refers to. For example, a school mailing list could be of parents of pupils—code 1, teachers on the staff—code 2, past pupils—code 3, and members of the governing body—code 4. It may be that under certain circumstances all people on the list will need to have their addresses printed. On other occasions it might only be a mailshot to parents. So there needs to be some sort of selection of parts of the list prior to printing out the sticky labels, which are then peeled off a continuous roll and affixed to envelopes. There must be the facility to add new names to and delete out-of-date names and addresses from the list. In addition, there needs to be some way that an entry in the list can be amended and finally the list needs to be sorted into surname order. This last facility is important because it is very easy—experience has shown this—to accidentally have the same name in the list several times or for each member of a household to have a separate entry.It is obviously a bad thing to have several copies of the same letter going to one house.

Our menu of options can be created as:

1. SELECT **number** FROM 5 CASES
2. CASE 1
3.  CHAIN SETUP
4. CASE 2
5.  CHAIN AMEND
6. CASE 3
7.  CHAIN SORT
8. CASE 4
9.  CHAIN PRINT
10.CASE 5
11. STOP
12.DEFAULT
13.  PRINT "Only the numbers 1,2,3,4 or 5 are acceptable"
14.SELECTEND

First of all we have to decide what each record has to look like and for this project we are going to allow for 10 fields in each record. These will be a title field—Mr, Mrs, etc.—an initials field, and a surname field. The address fields will be five in number, allowing for a house name, road name, town name, county, and postcode. The last two fields will be the telephone number and the print code field—the one which allows us to print selected sections of the list if required. This means that we can have all the records of about the same length with the various fields delimited by, say, the / character. For example, a typical entry might be :

Green/Mr/E.T./The Poplars/5 Garden Crescent/Luton/
Beds./LU6 4RT/45632/4/

Notice how the data have been stored in the record with the surname first. This is to make the records in the file easier to sort, since we will use the surname as the key on which to sort. In addition, once the records have been sorted into alphabetical order we can also use the surname as a key to search when we want to amend a particular record.

We could also use our mailing list for another purpose by extracting certain pieces of information from the entry to produce a list of telephone numbers so that not only would the program allow us to print

Mr E.T.Green
The Poplars
5 Garden Crescent
Luton
Beds
LU6 4RT

but also

Mr E.T.Green: Luton 45632

So let us amend our selection menu by adding a telephone list option:

```
1.  SELECT number FROM 6 CASES
2.  CASE 1
3.     CHAIN SETUP
4.  CASE 2
5.     CHAIN AMEND
6.  CASE 3
7.     CHAIN SORT
8.  CASE 4
9.     CHAIN PRINT
10. CASE 5
11.    CHAIN PHONE
12. CASE 6
13.    STOP
14. DEFAULT
15.    PRINT "Only the numbers 1,2,3,4,5 or 6 are acceptable"
16. SELECTEND
```

To start with we set up our list of names and addresses by saying:

1. Input the title, initials, and surname.
2. Input five address lines.
3. Input the telephone number and printing code.
4. Write this as a packed record with the fields separated by "/" characters.

So the SETUP program would look like this:

```
PROGRAM SETUP
1.  ARRAY address$ (1:5)
2.  PRINT "Title ?"
3.  READ title$
4.  LOOP
5.     PRINT "Initials ?"
6.     READ initials$
7.     PRINT "Surname ?"
8.     READ surname$
9.     LOOP FOR index=1 to 5
10.       PRINT "Address line ",index
11.       READ address$(index)
12.    REPEAT
13.    PRINT "Telephone number ?"
14.    READ telephone$
15.    PRINT "Printing code ?"
16.    READ code$
17.    LET record$:=surname$+"/"+title$+"/"+initials$+
          "/"+address$(1)+"/"+address$(2)+"/"+address$(3)+
          "/"+address$(4)+"/"+address$(5)+"/"+telephone$+
          "/"+code$+"/
18.    WRITE record$ to file
19.    PRINT "Title ?"
20     READ title$
21.REPEAT UNTIL title$="STOP"
22.RETURN TO MAIN MENU
```

An important subprogram would be one which decoded the surname from each record. This would be used in conjunction with the SORT program and the AMEND program since we would use these names as the keys to the records.

This program would search through each record until it comes across the first "/" character. All the characters to the left of that character make up the surname of the person. So we say:

1. Set **surname$** to be a blank.
2. Loop.
3.   Add characters to **surname$** one at a time.
4. Repeat until the next character read is "/".

```
SUBPROGRAM SURNAME(record$,surname$)
1.  LET surname$:=""
2.  LET index:=1
2.  LOOP
3.     LET surname$:=surname$+record$(index,1)
4.     LET index:=index+1
5.  REPEAT UNTIL record$(index,1)="/"
END OF SUBPROGRAM
```

The rest of the data held on each record can be decoded in exactly the same way by extracting the surname from each record and then putting the remaining data into a series of nine strings. The subprogram to completely decode the contents of a record would be:

```
SUBPROGRAM DECODE(record$,surname$,title$,initials$,
                  address$,telephone$,code$)
1.  ARRAY address$(1:5)
2.  ARRAY data$(1:9)
```

**92**

```
 3.  EXECUTE SURNAME(record$,surname$)
 4.  LET index:=lengthofsurname+2
 5.  LOOP
 6.    LOOP FOR counter=1 TO 9
 7.      LET data$(counter):=""
 8.      LOOP
 9.        LET data$(counter):=data$(counter)+record$(index,1)
10.        LET index:=index+1
11.      REPEAT UNTIL record$(index,1)="/"
12.    REPEAT
13.    LET index:=index+1
14.  REPEAT UNTIL index=lengthofrecord
15.LET title$:=data$(1)
16.LET initials$:=data$(2)
17.LOOP FOR index=1 TO 5
18.  LET address$(index)=data$(index+2)
19.REPEAT
20.LET telephone$:=data$(8)
21.LET code$:=data$(9)
END OF SUBPROGRAM
```

We have already written the SETUP program. Now we can write the AMEND program. In this we have to search for a particular record by name, amend it, or delete it as required and then return to the main menu. The record we wish to alter can be searched for in a number of ways. If the file is not very large a serial search is possible, but not very efficient. Alternatively, since the file is best arranged in alphabetical order, a search of the type described in Example 8 can be used using names instead of numbers. The search program can be written separately, of course, and will be referred to as the subprogram SEARCH, where a name is given to the subprogram which will return the record appropriate to that name.

Before we get down to our pseudo-code we can write:

1. Input a surname.
2. Search for the record with that surname.
3. Decode the contents of the record.
4. Print the contents of the record.
5. Enquire if the record is to be deleted.
6. If the record is to be deleted.
7.    Then replace the record with a blank.
8.    Else input the amendments and write the amended record back to its original place.
9. Ifend.

```
PROGRAM AMEND
1.  ARRAY address$(1:5)
2.  WRITE "Name to be searched for in mailing list ?"
3.  READ name$
4.  LOOP
5.    EXECUTE SEARCH(name$,record$)
```

```
6.     EXECUTE DECODE(record$,surname$,title$,initials$,
                       address$,telephone$,code$)
7.     PRINT title$,initials$,surname$
8.     PRINT address$(1),"Entry 1"
9.     PRINT address$(2),"Entry 2"
10.    PRINT address$(3),"Entry 3"
11.    PRINT address$(4),"Entry 4"
12.    PRINT address$(5),"Entry 5"
13.    PRINT telephone$
14.    PRINT code$
15.    PRINT "Is the entry O.K.?"
16.    READ answer$
17.    IF answer$="NO"
18.       THEN
19.          PRINT "Is the whole entry to be deleted ?"
20.          READ reply$
21.         IF reply$="YES"
22.            THEN
23.               LET record$:=""
24.               WRITE record$ TO record just read
25.            ELSE
26.               PRINT "Title"
27.               READ title1$
28.               IF title1$<>""
29.                  THEN
30.                     LET title$:=title1$
31.                  ELSE
32.                     SKIP
33.               IFEND
34.               PRINT "Initials"
35.               READ initials1$
36.               IF initials1$<>""
37.                  THEN
38.                     LET initials$:=initials1$
39.                  ELSE
40.                     SKIP
41.               IFEND
42.               PRINT "Surname"
43.               READ surname1$
44.               IF surname1$<>""
45.                  THEN
46.                     LET surname$:=surname1$
47.                  ELSE
48.                     SKIP
49.               IFEND
50.               LOOP FOR index=1 to 5
51.                  PRINT "Address line",index
52.                  READ newline$
53.                  IF newline$<>""
54.                     THEN
55.                        LETaddress$(index):=newline$
56.                     ELSE
57.                        SKIP
58.                  IFEND
59.               REPEAT
60.               PRINT "Telephone No:"
61.               READ telephone1$
62.               IF telephone1$<>""
63.                  THEN
64.                     LET telephone$:=telephone1$
65.                  ELSE
66.                     SKIP
67.               IFEND
68.               PRINT "Printing code"
69.               READ code1$
70.               IF code1$<>""
71.                  THEN
72.                     LET code$:=code1$
73.                  ELSE
74.               IFEND
```

**94**

```
75.              LET record$:=surname$+"/"+title$+"/"+initials$+
          "/"+address$(1)+"/"+address$(2)+"/"+address$(3)+
          "/"+address$(4)+"/"+address$(5)+"/"+telephone$+
          "/"+code$+"/
76.              WRITE record$ TO record just read
77.          IFEND
78.          READ name$
79.  REPEAT UNTIL name$="STOP"
80.  RETURN TO MAIN MENU
```

Once again the SQUASH routine can be used to eliminate unwanted records from the file.

The SORT program can be any one of the various methods of sorting which you may know. As a start there are several methods suggested to you in the examples earlier in the text which will be quite straightforward. The PRINT program will be very short and will look like this:

1. Enquire if all entries are to be printed.
2. If all are to be printed
3. Then print the contents of each record in the form of a label followed by spaces.
4. Else input the printing key. Then print those records with that printing key in the form of a label followed by spaces.
5. Ifend.

```
PROGRAM PRINT
1.  ARRAY address(1:5)
2.  PRINT "Do you wish to print all the entries in the
    mailing list ?"
3.  READ reply$
4.  IF reply$="YES"
5.    THEN
6.       LOOP WHILE there are records to be read
7.          READ record$ FROM the current record
8.          EXECUTE DECODE(record$,surname$,title$,initals$,
                          address$,telephone$,code$)
9.          PRINT title$,initials$,surname$
10.         PRINT address$(1)
11.         PRINT address$(2)
12.         PRINT address$(3)
13.         PRINT address$(4)
14.         PRINT address$(5)
15.         PRINT SPACES
16.         PRINT SPACES
17.      REPEAT
18.    ELSE
19.       PRINT "Which code do you want to print ?"
20.       READ type$
21.       LOOP WHILE there are records to be read
22.          READ record$ FROM the current record
23.          EXECUTE DECODE(record$,surname$,title$,initals$,
                          address$,telephone$,code$)
24.          IF type$=code$
25.             THEN
26.                PRINT title$,initials$,surname$
27.                PRINT address$(1)
28.                PRINT address$(2)
29.                PRINT address$(3)
30.                PRINT address$(4)
31.                PRINT address$(5)
```

```
32.              PRINT SPACES
33.              PRINT SPACES
34.        ELSE
35.            SKIP
36.        IFEND
37.     REPEAT
38.IFEND
39.RETURN TO MAIN MENU
```

The program to print the telephone numbers is really very
similar to the above program but with lines 9 to 16 replaced
with:

```
9. PRINT title$,initials$,surname$,":",telephone$
10.PRINT SPACES
```

and similarly for lines 26 to 33.

## Project 4—Curve of best fit

This is a project which should appeal to the more mathematically
minded. It also goes to demonstrate that good programming
techniques can be applied to programs which do not have
anything to do with business and finance. In fact, it is true to
say that the first practical uses of computers were in the field of
mathematics, which is why many of the computers in use today
in educational institutions are still firmly fixed in departments
of mathematics and science. The problem to be dealt with here
concerns the derivation of the equation of that curve which best
fits a set of pairs of points obtained as the result of experimental
observations. This means that we should end up with the
equation of the curve which can be drawn to smooth out
inaccuracies of man-made observations. It can be shown by
some complicated mathematics, which will not be dealt with
here, that the best curves to fit a set of points obtained from
experimental data will be either of a quadratic form,

$$y = Ax^2 + Bx + C$$

or an exponential form,

$$y = Ae^{Bx}$$

In the program there will be two subprograms, called QUAD
and EXPO, which will be listed after the main program. The
program will produce the equation of the curve of best fit and a
table of the results reached by the initial experiment, followed
by the values obtained by using the calculated equation and the
difference between the two. It should be noted that, as in

**96**

general for this kind of work, the x values, usually called the **independent** variables, are deemed to be accurate. The y values, called the **dependent** variables, are the ones obtained by observation and are those which are likely to be in error. It is these values which are recalculated from the equation given by the program and compared with the originals. It can then be seen whether the quadratic equation or the exponential equation gives the better fit. The method in fact consists of summing combinations of the pairs of x and y values, setting up a set of simultaneous equations and then solving them. This is done by a matrix method which is by far the best way of getting a computer to solve this sort of problem since the method is capable of expansion to cover any number of sets of equations.

The top-down approach to the solution of the problem is quite straightforward and looks like this:

1. Read in the pairs of x and y values.
2. Decide whether the quadratic or exponential curve is to be tried out.
3. If the exponential curve is to be tried then replace each y value by its logarithm.
4. Sum all the x values.
5. Sum the squares of the x values.
6. Sum the cubes of the x values.
7. Sum the fourth powers of the x values.
8. Sum the y values.
9. Sum the products of each x value and its corresponding y value.
10. Sum the products of each x value and the square of its corresponding y value.
11. Place the number of pairs of values and the results from 4 and 5 in the first row of a table.
12. Place the results from 4,5, and 6 in the second row of a table.
13. Place the results from 5,6, and 7 in the third row of a table.
14. Place the results from 8,9, and 10 into a list.
15. If the quadratic form is wanted, evaluate the quadratic curve of best fit.
16. If the exponential form is wanted, evaluate the exponential curve of best fit.

In pseudo-code this becomes:

```
1. ARRAY n(1:4,1:4)
2. ARRAY k(1:4)
3. ARRAY x(1:50)
4. ARRAY y(1:50)
```

```
5.  ARRAY z(1:50)
6.  PRINT "How many pairs of points ?"
7.  READ number
8.  LOOP FOR index=1 to number
9.     READ x(index)
10.    READ z(index)
11. REPEAT
12. PRINT "Choose Quadratic (1) or Exponential (2)"
13. READ type
14. IF type=1
15.    THEN
16.       LOOP FOR index=1 to number
17.          LET y(index)=LOG(z(index))
18.       REPEAT
19.    ELSE
20.       LOOP FOR index=1 to number
21.          y(index)=z(index)
22.       REPEAT
23. IFEND
24. LET xr1:=0
25. LET xr2:=0
26. LET xr3:=0
27. LET xr4:=0
28. LET xyr1:=0
29. LET xyr2:=0
30. LET yr:=0
31. LOOP FOR index=1 to number
32.    LET xr1:=xr1+x(index)
33.    LET xr2:=xr2+x(index)*x(index)
34.    LET xr3:=xr3+x(index)*x(index)*x(index)
35.    LET xr4:=xr4+x(index)*x(index)*x(index)*x(index)
36.    LET yr:=yr+y(index)
37.    LET xyr1:=xyr1+x(index)*y(index)
38.    LET xyr2:=xyr2+x(index)*x(index)*y(index)
39. REPEAT
40. LET n(1,1):=number
41. LET n(1,2):=xr1
42. LET n(1,3):=xr2
43. LET n(2,1):=xr1
44. LET n(2,2):=xr2
45. LET n(2,3):=xr3
46. LET n(3,1):=xr2
47. LET n(3,2):=xr3
48. LET n(3,3):=xr4
49. LET k(1):=yr1
50. LET k(2):=xyr1
51. LET k(3):=xyr2
52. IF type=1
53.    THEN
54.       EXECUTE QUAD(n,k,number,x,y)
55.    ELSE
56.       EXECUTE EXPO(n,k,number,x,y)
57. IFEND
58. END
```

Now for the two subprograms. Both of these work in the same manner. They each solve a set of simultaneous equations whose coefficients are held in the table set up in the main program and whose right-hand side is held in the list set up in the main program. The solution is obtained by inverting the matrix of the coefficients and then multiplying the resulting matrix by the column matrix which is the list of constants. The two subprograms follow the same pattern:

1.  Invert the matrix.

**98**

2. Multiply the matrix by the list.
3. The resulting list contains the coefficients of the variables in the required equations.
4. Recalculate the values of y for each of the x values according to the equation derived.
5. Compare each of the calculated values with the observed y values and print them out.

The subprogram QUAD uses a mathematical function known as MOD. This is the remainder obtained when one number is divided by another. For example, if we write MOD(5,2) we get 1—which is the remainder obtained when 5 is divided by 2. Similarly, MOD(7,4) gives 3.

```
SUBPROGRAM QUAD(n,k,number,x,y)
1.  ARRAY n1(1:4,1:4)
2.  ARRAY pt(1:4)
3.  LET det:=n(1,1)*(n(2,2)*n(3,3)-n(2,3)*n(3,2))
              -n(1,2)*(n(2,1)*n(3,3)-n(2,3)*n(3,1))
              +n(1,3)*(n(2,1)*n(3,2)-n(2,2)*n(3,1))
4.  LOOP FOR index=1 to 3
5.     LET i1:=MOD(index,3)+1
6.     LET i2:=MOD(i1,3)+1
7.     LOOP FOR index1=1 to 3
8.        LET j1:=MOD(index1,3)+1
9.        LET j2:=MOD(j1,3)+1
10.       LET n1(index1,index):=(n(i1,j1)*n(i2,j2)
                    -n(i1,j2)*n(i2,j1))/det
11.    REPEAT
12.REPEAT
13.LOOP FOR index=1 to 3
14.    LET pti:=0
15.    LOOP FOR index1=1 to 3
16.       LET pti:=pti+n1(index,index1)*k(index2)
17.    REPEAT
18.    LET pt(index):=pti
19.REPEAT
20.PRINT "The equation is :-"
21.PRINT "Y = ",pt(1),"+",pt(2),"X +",pt(3),"X*X"
22.LOOP FOR index=1 to number
23.    LET calc:=pt(1)+pt(2)*x(index)+pt(3)*x(index)*x(index)
24.    LET diff:=y(index)-calc
25.    PRINT x(index),y(index),calc,diff
26.REPEAT
END OF SUBPROGRAM
```

The subprogram called EXPO calculates the equation of the best exponential curve which fits the points. Note that it only uses a 2 x 2 matrix for the coefficients and a list with two entries. This is because there are only two unknowns in the exponential equation and hence only a pair of simultaneous equations to solve. The quadratic curve has three coefficients to be calculated and so three sets of equations have to be solved in QUAD.

```
SUBPROGRAM EXPO(n,k,number,x,y)
1.  ARRAY pt(1:4)
2.  LET det:=n(1,1)*n(2,2)-n(2,1)*n(1,2)
```

```
 3. LET n(1,2):=-n(1,2)
 4. LET n(2,1):=-n(2,1)
 5. LET temp:=n(1,1)
 6. LET n(1,1):=n(2,2)
 7. LET n(2,2):=temp
 8. LET n(1,1):=n(1,1)/det
 9. LET n(1,2):=n(1,2)/det
10.LET n(2,1):=n(2,1)/det
11.LET n(2,2):=n(2,2)/det
12.LET pt(1):=n(1,1)*k(1)*n(1,2)*k(2)
13.LET pt(2):=n(2,1)*k(1)*n(1,2)*k(2)
14.LET exp:=EXP(pt(1))
15.PRINT "The equation is :-"
16.PRINT "Y = exp * EXP(",pt(2),"*X)"
17.LOOP FOR index:=1 to number
18.   LET y(index):=EXP(y(index))
19.   LET calc:=exp*EXP(pt(2)*x(index))
20.   LET diff:=y(index)-calc
21.   PRINT x(index),y(index),calc,diff
22.REPEAT
END OF SUBPROGRAM
```

As it stands this is a program which works, and works very satisfactorily. What is a disadvantage is that the output from it is purely numerical and the graph which is the ultimate aim of the whole exercise has to be drawn manually from the tables which the program produces. The program would be even more useful if it could be expanded by adding a graph-plotting routine after plotting the table. This is not really difficult since the output is in the form of a function which can then be used to plot a graph. In other words, we could add a line to QUAD which reads:

```
19a. DEFINE FUNCTION F(x)=pt(1)+pt(2)*x+pt(3)*x*x
```

and an extra line to EXPO which reads:

```
14a. DEFINE FUNCTION F(x)=exp*EXP(pt(2)*x)
```

Then another subprogram, GRAPH, could be called which plots the graph. How this does it depends a lot on the type of machine you are using and the graph-plotting facilities available to you. What needs to be given to GRAPH is the definition of the function to be plotted and the range of x values of the original results. Then the subprogram can go ahead and plot the graph. Because of the great variation of graph-plotting facilities available only a broad outline of the process is given and it will be up to the reader to provide a detailed program specific to the machine being used. Basically, a program such as this will need to draw a pair of axes, x axis horizontal and y axis vertical,and mark them off with suitable scales. Because the range of x values is known this range can be divided into an appropriate number of steps and the corresponding y values calculated according to the calculated function. Then each point can be drawn. If required, the original

**100**

set of pairs of points can be plotted on the same pair of axes so that a comparison of observed and calculated values can be made and goodness of fit can be checked. An outline of the subprogram would therefore look something like this:

```
SUBPROGRAM GRAPH(FUNCTION F(x),x,y,number)
1.  Ask for the increments of x to be plotted
2.  Ask for initial and final values of x
3.  Calculate the range of values of x
4.  Calculate the range of values of y
5.  Draw x and y axes
6.  Label and scale the axes
7.  LOOP FOR increment of x FROM initial TO final values
8.     Calculate y-value from x-value
9.     Calculate coordinates on graph for x-value
       and y-value
10.    PRINT "*" at appropriate position
11. REPEAT
12. LOOP FOR index=1 number
13.    Calculate coordinates on graph for x(index)
       and y(index)
13.    PRINT "x" at appropriate position
14. REPEAT
END OF SUBPROGRAM
```

This subprogram only plots points, since most microcomputers will do this with ease. If an actual graph needs to be plotted then some form of DRAW command would be used to make the computer join up a pair of points. GRAPH could then be inserted at the end of each of the subprograms QUAD and EXPO. In QUAD we would add:

```
27. PRINT "Do you want a graph of this ?"
28. READ reply$
29. IF reply$="YES"
30.    THEN
31.       EXECUTE GRAPH(FUNCTION F(x),x,y,number)
32.    ELSE
33.       SKIP
34. IFEND
```

and similarly in EXPO we would add the same sequence from line 23 onwards.

So here we have a fairly high-powered mathematical problem programmed using the structured approach. Notice how we have been able to add parts to the program and write sections quite separately which then can be incorporated not only into this program but into others as well.

## Project 5—Keeping track of hire cars

This project shows how we can organize and maintain a fleet of hire cars with a computer program which can run on computers of quite modest size. An operator who runs a hire fleet has to be able to obtain certain information about his fleet quickly and be able to modify this information easily. He needs, for example, to be able to list all the cars in his fleet, list all those that are available for hire, list all those which are presently on hire, and ensure that his cars are maintained on a regular basis. All this points to the necessity of keeping a list of the cars with all the details of each car's current status. At first one would expect that this would require a series of lists: one for the total fleet, one for those on hire, one for those being serviced, and so on. Then the data about each car would be moved about from list to list. This proves to be very cumbersome and there are better ways.One way of handling such data is to have one list only, but use it for a number of purposes. For example, suppose the fleet consisted of four types of car only. These are coded as follows:

| | Type | Code |
|---|---|---|
| 1300 | Escort | A |
| 1600 | Escort | B |
| 1300 | Cavalier | C |
| 1600 | Cavalier | D |

The first entry for each vehicle in the table below is its type code. Following this will be its registration number,the number of hours' work to be carried out at its next service, the mileage when the next service is due, its current mileage, and four more fields. These fields are known as 'pointers' and are used to separate the one list into four lists. The four fields contain pointers for the availability list, the on-hire list, the awaiting service list, and the being serviced list. First of all we have to store a list of four numbers which tell us the table entry number of the record at the head of each list. In the example table shown the first car on the availability list is number 2, the first car in the on-hire list is number 3, the first car awaiting service is number 7, and the first car on the list of those being serviced is number 8. If we look at the entry in column 6 for record 2 we see that it is 6. This tells us that the next car in the availability list is number 6 and if we look at number 6 we see that the one to follow that in the list is number 18, and so on until finally we reach number 4 which has -1 in the pointer field. This indicates that this record is the last one in the list. The same applies to the on-hire list, which starts with number 3, which points to number 1, then to number 5, and then to number 10. The last entry in this list is number 99 where again the number -1 tells us that the end of the list has been reached. The same procedure applies to the other two lists.

Pointers: P(1):2
         P(2):3
         P(3):7
         P(4):8

| | type | reg | hours | nextserv | mileage | avail | hire | awserv | serv |
|---|---|---|---|---|---|---|---|---|---|
| 1. | A | RGT417Y | 3 | 45000 | 40000 | 0 | 5 | 0 | 0 |
| 2. | B | PBA47X | 6 | 50000 | 47000 | 6 | 0 | 0 | 0 |
| 3. | C | UTL789X | 5 | 60000 | 53500 | 0 | 1 | 0 | 0 |
| 4. | D | PBY45X | 6 | 30000 | 29000 | -1 | 0 | 0 | 0 |
| 5. | A | DRA123W | 3 | 70000 | 64000 | 0 | 10 | 0 | 0 |
| 6. | D | WEW722X | 6 | 12000 | 11000 | 18 | 0 | 0 | 0 |
| 7. | A | PER43Y | 3 | 12500 | 12000 | 0 | 0 | 20 | 0 |
| 8. | B | JVG422X | 6 | 30650 | 30000 | 0 | 0 | 0 | 14 |
| 9....... | | | | | | | | | |
| 10...... | | | | | | | | | |
| : | | | | | | | | | |
| 97...... | | | | | | | | | |
| 98...... | | | | | | | | | |
| 99. | A | PBR211X | 6 | 48000 | 45600 | 0 | -1 | 0 | 0 |
| 100. | B | TYG47Y | 3 | 24000 | 23500 | 4 | 0 | 0 | 0 |

Amending the lists becomes a matter of changing the pointers so that each list can be read in the order dictated by the appropriate pointers. If we hold the details of each car in a string we can separate the various fields by a * symbol so that we would have

**A\*RGT657Y\*3\*45000\*41000\*3\*0\*0\*0\***

as a typical entry. Only one of the last four fields contains a number, the three zeros telling us that the vehicle is not on the lists which use those pointers.

First of all let us have a subprogram which decodes the data held in one record:

1. Set up a list with nine entries.
2. Loop for a count of 1 to 9.
3.    Place a blank in the entry.
4.    Scan through the record character by character.

5.   Place each character into the entry
6.   Until the character read is a "*".
7. Repeat.
8. Allocate an appropriate character string to the **type$** field.
9. Allocate **reg$,hours$**, etc., to the remaining eight entries in the list.

```
SUBPROGRAM DECODE(record$,type$,reg$,hours$,nextserv$,
                  miles$,avail$,hire$,await$,service$)
1.ARRAY rec$(1:9)
2.LET index:=0
3.LOOP FOR count=1 to 9
4.   LET rec$(count):=""
5.   LET index:=index+1
6.   LOOP
7.     LET rec$(count):=rec$(count)+record$(index)
8.     LET index:=index+1
9.   REPEAT UNTIL record$(index)="*"
10.REPEAT
11.IF rec$(1)="A"
12.   THEN
13.     LET type$:="1300 Escort"
14.   ELSE
15.     IF rec$(1)="B"
16.       THEN
17.         LET type$:="1600 Escort"
18.       ELSE
19.         IF rec$(1)="C"
20.           THEN
21.             LET type$:="1300 Cavalier"
22.           ELSE
23.             IF rec$(1)="D"
24.               THEN
25.                 LET type$:="1600 Cavalier"
26.               ELSE
27.                 SKIP
29.             IFEND
30.           IFEND
31.       IFEND
32.IFEND
33.LET reg$:=rec$(2)
34.LET hours$:=rec$(3)
35.LET nextserv$:=rec$(4)
36.LET miles$:=rec$(5)
37.LET avail$:=rec$(6)
37.LET hire$:=rec$(7)
38.LET await$:=rec$(8)
39.LET service$:=rec$(9)
END OF SUBPROGRAM
```

A program which will print out any one of the four lists would simply have to pick up the number of the record at the head of the list and then use this to read the record with that number. In that record will be the pointer which gives the number of the next record in the sequence which follows. The program then continues to thread through the table until it reaches a pointer field which is -1, which indicates that the end of that list has been reached. A program which will print out the contents of any one of the four lists would be like this:

1. Input the list identifier.
2. Extract the appropriate starting record number from the pointer list.
3. Call the record number **next**.
4. Loop.
5. Decode record(**next**) from the list of cars.
6. Set **next** to the appropriate field of record.
7. Print the car type and registration number.
8. Repeat until **next**=-1.

```
PROGRAM PRINT
1.  ARRAY cars$ (1:100)
2.  ARRAY pointers (1:4)
3.  PRINT "Which list do you want to print out ?"
4.  PRINT "Type 1 for list of available cars"
5.  PRINT "Type 2 for list of cars on hire"
6.  PRINT "Type 3 for list of cars awaiting service"
7.  PRINT "Type 4 for list of cars being serviced"
8.  READ number
9.  LET next:=pointers(number)
10.LOOP
11.    LET record$:=cars$(next)
12.    EXECUTE DECODE(record$,type$,reg$,hours$,nextserv$,
                      miles$,avail$,hire$,await$,service$)
13.    IF number=1
14.      THEN
15.        LET next:=avail$
16.      ELSE
17.        IF number=2
18.          THEN
19.            LET next:=hire$
20.          ELSE
21.            IF number=3
22.              THEN
23.                LET next:=await$
24.              ELSE
25.                IF number=4
26.                  THEN
27.                    LET next:=service$
28.                  ELSE
29.                    SKIP
30.                IFEND
31.            IFEND
32.        IFEND
33.    IFEND
34.    PRINT type$,"Reg No:",reg$
35.REPEAT UNTIL next=-1
RETURN TO MAIN MENU
```

We can use a version of this program to search through the table in order to find out if a car of a particular type is available.

```
SUBPROGRAM AVAIL(code$,reply$)
1.  ARRAY cars$ (1:100)
2.  ARRAY pointers (1:4)
3.  IF code$="A"
4.    THEN
5.      LET code$:="1300 Escort"
6.    ELSE
7.      IF code$="B"
8.        THEN
9.          LET code$:="1600 Escort"
10.       ELSE
11.         IF code$="C"
```

```
12.              THEN
13.                 LET code$:="1300 Cavalier"
14.              ELSE
15.                 IF code$="D"
16.                    THEN
17.                       LET code$:="1600 Cavalier"
18.                    ELSE
19.                       SKIP
20.                 IFEND
21.           IFEND
22.      IFEND
23.IFEND
24.LET next:=pointers(1)
25.LET any:=0
26.LOOP
27.   LET record$:=cars$(next)
28.   EXECUTE DECODE(record$,type$,reg$,hours$,nextserv$,
                     miles$,avail$,hire$,await$,service$)
29.   IF code$=type$
30.      THEN
31.         PRINT type$,reg$,"available. Car number:",next
32.         LET any:=1
33.      ELSE
34.         SKIP
35.   IFEND
36.   LET next:=avail$
37.REPEAT UNTIL next=-1
38.IF any=0
39.   THEN
40.      LET reply$:="No vehicles of this type available"
41.   ELSE
42.      LET reply$:="The above vehicles are available"
43.IFEND
END OF SUBPROGRAM
```

If a car of a particular type is seen to be available then it must be taken off the available list and placed on the hire list when it goes out on hire. This will require a program called HIRE which will amend the appropriate pointers in the two lists. When the car is returned its mileage must be checked to see if it is due for service. If it is, then before it is placed back on the available list it goes onto the awaiting service list, after which it is serviced. On completion of the service it can be placed back onto the list of cars available for hire, with the mileage before the next service amended in the main table:

1. Input the list number of the car to be hired.
2. If the car to be hired is at the head of the list
3. Then place the car with that reference on the end of the 'hired' list, i.e., place -1 into its **hire$** field and zeros in the other link fields.
4. Write the **avail$** pointer into the first item of the **pointers** list.
5. Reassemble the record and write it back into the **cars** list.
6. Go to the head of the 'hire' list.
7. Read through the 'hire' list until the record with -1 in its link field is found.

**106**

8. Replace its **hire$** field with the record number of the car just hired.
9. Reassemble the record and write it back into the **cars** list.
10. Else read through the list of cars starting with the one at the head of the list until the **avail$** field is the record number required.
11. Place -1 in the **hire$** field of that record and zeros in the other link fields.
12. Reassemble the record and write it back into the **cars** list.
13. Place the **avail$** field in the **avail$** field of the record which pointed to that record.
14. Reassemble the record and write it back into the **cars** list.
15. Read through the 'hire' list until the record with -1 in its link field is found.
16. Replace its **hire$** field with the record number of the car just hired.
17. Reassemble the record and write it back into the **cars** list.
18. Ifend.

Some examples should help here. The first shows the state of affairs before number 3 car goes out on hire:

| | type | reg | hours | nextserv | mileage | avail | hire | awserv | serv |
|---|---|---|---|---|---|---|---|---|---|
| 1. | A | RGV457T | 3 | 40000 | 35000 | 3 | 0 | 0 | 0 |
| 2. | C | THG439X | 6 | 45000 | 42000 | 0 | 5 | 0 | 0 |
| 3. | B | AAV321X | 3 | 30000 | 28000 | 4 | 0 | 0 | 0 |
| 4. | A | TYH23Y | 3 | 12000 | 8000 | -1 | 0 | 0 | 0 |
| 5. | D | ERA234W | 6 | 40000 | 35000 | 0 | -1 | 0 | 0 |
| 6..... | | | | | | | | | |
| 7..... | | | | | | | | | |

The **pointers** list contains the numbers 1, 2, 8 and 7. If car number 3 is to be hired our table will have to become:

| | type | reg | hours | nextserv | mileage | avail | hire | awserv | serv |
|---|---|---|---|---|---|---|---|---|---|
| 1. | A | RGV453T | 3 | 40000 | 35000 | 4 | 0 | 0 | 0 |
| 2. | C | THG439X | 6 | 45000 | 42000 | 0 | 5 | 0 | 0 |
| 3. | B | AAV321X | 3 | 30000 | 28000 | 0 | -1 | 0 | 0 |
| 4. | A | TYH23Y | 3 | 12000 | 8000 | -1 | 0 | 0 | 0 |
| 5. | D | ERA234W | 6 | 40000 | 35000 | 0 | 3 | 0 | 0 |

showing that car number 3 has been added onto the end of the list of cars on hire and taken out of the available list. If car number 1 were wanted then the table would become:

| | type | reg | hours | nextserv | mileage | avail | hire | awserv | serv |
|---|---|---|---|---|---|---|---|---|---|
| 1. | A | RGV453T | 3 | 40000 | 35000 | 0 | -1 | 0 | 0 |
| 2. | C | THG439X | 6 | 45000 | 42000 | 0 | 5 | 0 | 0 |
| 3. | B | AAV321X | 3 | 30000 | 28000 | 0 | 1 | 0 | 0 |
| 4. | A | TYH23Y | 3 | 12000 | 8000 | -1 | 0 | 0 | 0 |
| 5. | D | ERA234W | 6 | 40000 | 35000 | 0 | 3 | 0 | 0 |

and the **pointers** list would also be amended to become 4, 2, 8, and 7.

```
PROGRAM HIRE
1.  ARRAY cars$(1:100)
2.  ARRAY pointers(1:4)
3.  ARRAY rec1$(1:9)
4.  PRINT "Type in the reference number of the car to be
           hired"
5.  READ number
6.  IF number=pointers(1)
7.    THEN
8.      LET record$:=cars$(number)
9.      EXECUTE DECODE(record$,type$,reg$,hours$,nextserv$,
                      miles$,avail$,hire$,await$,service$)
10.     LET rec1$(1):=type$
11.     LET rec1$(2):=reg$
12.     LET rec1$(3):=hours$
13.     LET rec1$(4):=nextserv$
14.     LET rec1$(5):=miles$
15.     LET rec1$(6):="0"
16.     LET rec1$(7):="-1"
17.     LET rec1$(8):="0"
18.     LET rec1$(9):="0"
19.     LET pointers(1):=avail$
20.     LET record$:=""
21.     LOOP FOR index=1 to 9
22.        LET record$:=record$+rec1$(index)+"*"
23.     REPEAT
24.     LET cars$(number):=record$
25.     LET next:=pointers(2)
26.     LOOP
27.        LET record$:=cars$(next)
28.        LET hold:=next
29.        EXECUTE DECODE(record$,type$,reg$,hours$,nextserv$,
                         miles$,avail$,hire$,await$,service$)
30.        LET next:=hire$
31.     REPEAT UNTIL next=-1
32.     LET rec1$(1):=type$
33.     LET rec1$(2):=reg$
34.     LET rec1$(3):=hours$
35      LET rec1$(4):=nextserv$
36.     LET rec1$(5):=miles$
37.     LET rec1$(6):="0"
38.     LET rec1$(7):=number
39.     LET rec1$(8):="0"
40.     LET rec1$(9):="0"
41.     LET record$:=""
42.     LOOP FOR index=1 to 9
43.        LET record$:=record$+rec1$(index)+"*"
44.     REPEAT
45.     LET cars$(hold):=record$
46.   ELSE
47.     LET next:=pointers(1)
48.     LOOP
```

```
49.       LET record$:=cars$(next)
50.       LET hold:=next
51.       EXECUTE DECODE(record$,type$,reg$,hours$,nextserv$,
                 miles$,avail$,hire$,await$,service$)
52.       LET next:=avail$
53.     REPEAT UNTIL next=number
54.     LET record$:=cars$(next)
55.     EXECUTE DECODE(record$,type$,reg$,hours$,nextserv$,
                 miles$,avail$,hire$,await$,service$)
56.     LET rec1$(1):=type$
57.     LET rec1$(2):=reg$
58.     LET rec1$(3):=hours$
59.     LET rec1$(4):=nextserv$
60.     LET rec1$(5):=miles$
61.     LET rec1$(6):="0"
62.     LET rec1$(7):="-1"
63.     LET rec1$(8):="0"
64.     LET rec1$(9):="0"
65.     LET record$:=""
66.     LOOP FOR index=1 to 9
67.       LET record$:=record$+rec1$(index)+"*"
68.     REPEAT
70.     LET cars$(next):=record$
71.     LET record$:=cars$(hold)
72.     LET avail1$:=avail$
73.     EXECUTE DECODE(record$,type$,reg$,hours$,nextserv$,
                 miles$,avail$,hire$,await$,service$)
74.     LET rec1$(1):=type$
75.     LET rec1$(2):=reg$
76.     LET rec1$(3):=hours$
77.     LET rec1$(4):=nextserv$
78.     LET rec1$(5):=miles$
79.     LET rec1$(6):=avail1$
80.     LET rec1$(7):="0"
81.     LET rec1$(8):="0"
82.     LET rec1$(9):="0"
83.     LET record$:=""
84.     LOOP FOR index=1 to 9
85.       LET record$:=record$+rec1$(index)+"*"
86.     REPEAT
87.     LET cars$(hold):=record
88.     LET next:=pointers(2)
89.     LOOP
90.       LET record$:=cars$(next)
91.       LET hold:=next
92.       EXECUTE DECODE(record$,type$,reg$,hours$,nextserv$,
                 miles$,avail$,hire$,await$,service$)
93.       LET next:=hire$
94.     REPEAT UNTIL next=-1
95.     LET rec1$(1):=type$
96.     LET rec1$(2):=reg$
97.     LET rec1$(3):=hours$
98      LET rec1$(4):=nextserv$
99.     LET rec1$(5):=miles$
100.    LET rec1$(6):="0"
101.    LET rec1$(7):=number
102.    LET rec1$(8):="0"
103.    LET rec1$(9):="0"
104.    LET record$:=""
105.    LOOP FOR index=1 to 9
106.      LET record$:=record$+rec1$(index)+"*"
107.    REPEAT
108.      LET cars$(hold):=record$
109. IFEND
```

The menu of options for this project would allow for the
PRINT and the HIRE options already dealt with. What are also
needed are programs to receive a car back from hire, to place it

on the list of cars awaiting service if necessary or to place it back on the hire list, to transfer a car from the awaiting service list to the servicing list, and to transfer a car back onto the available list after having been serviced:

1.  SELECT **number** FROM 6 CASES
2.  CASE 1
3.    CHAIN PRINT
4.  CASE 2
5.    CHAIN HIRE
6.  CASE 3
7.    CHAIN RETURN
8.  CASE 4
9.    CHAIN RETURNTOHIRE
10. CASE 5
11.   STOP
12. DEFAULT
13.   PRINT "Only the numbers 1,2,3,4, or 5 are acceptable"
14. SELECTEND

The RETURN program will require to know the car number and the current mileage so that the program can decide whether to return the car to the available list if its mileage has not reached that of its next service or to place the car on the list of those awaiting servicing. Finally, when the RETURNTOHIRE program is run the car is taken from the servicing list and placed back onto the available list with the mileage to the next service field amended; then the next car on the list of those awaiting service will be transferred from the waiting list to the servicing list.

Since the RETURN program and the RETURNTOHIRE program are so very similar to those already written it will be left as an exercise for the reader to develop them. This system could be used in other situations of a similar nature, e.g., a video hire library.

## Project 6—A bar stock problem

This problem could, of course, be adapted to many situations where a small organization maintains a stock of a series of items whose numbers are never constant. The stock of the bar of a small hotel or club, for example, will change from day to day as stock is sold and replenished. The deliveries tend to be on a fairly regular basis, perhaps weekly, and a close watch has to be

**110**

kept on the value of the stock in case too much is held of a slow-moving item or not enough is held to take sudden spurts of trade into account. The actual counting of stock is a tedious enough job but when the calculation of the value of the stock has to be done as well the whole task can become very time-consuming, hence it is generally not done as often as it might be. This is where a computer program of the sort shortly to be detailed comes in very handy. Again, like the others in this book, it can be run on a machine of modest size— even without a disk drive if need be.

First of all we have to decide what data we need relating to each stock item and how this is to be stored. Although there might be a mass of potentially useful data which we could have, let us just keep it to the basic necessities. These are a description of each stock item together with its size, the cost of each unit purchased, the number of bottles in stock, the number of bottles in each unit, and the date of the last purchase of that item. Although the word 'bottles' has been used we could just as well refer to 'bags' or 'cards' since most bars sell bags of crisps and cards of packets of nuts as well as bottles of beer. The idea of the unit is important since very few things are bought singly; more usually they are bought by the crate or the case.

For this problem it is probably best to store the data in fixed length records,as described in the introductory section to these projects. Let us decide on a fixed record length of 51 characters. We can divide these up as follows:

Name:25 characters (characters 1 – 25)
Bottle size:10 characters (characters 26 – 35)
Unit cost:5 characters (characters 36 – 40)
Number of bottles in stock:3 characters
                    (characters 41 – 43)
Number of bottles per unit:3 characters
                    (characters 44 – 46)
Date of last purchase: 5 characters (in the form of year no. and day no.) (characters 47 – 51)

So a typical entry might be:

```
Bloggs Dinner Ale       half-pint  9.60102 4882308
. . . . . . . . . . . . . . . . . . . . . . . .!. . . . . . . . . . .!. . . .!. .!. .!. . . .!
1                              25        35  40 43 46    51
```

telling us that the stock of Bloggs Dinner Ale, half-pints,

costing £9.60 per case of 48, stands at 102 bottles and the last delivery was made on the 308th day of 1982, namely November. Likewise:

```
Strowgers Best Bitter    9-gallons 25.60108 7282354
........................!..........!....!..!..!....!
1                        25         35   40 43 46   51
```

tells us that the stock of Strowgers Best Bitter, in 9–gallon barrels, which cost £25.60 each, stands at 108 pints (one and a half barrels). The last delivery was made on day 354 of 1982—20 December.

Assuming we have a table containing details of, say, 200 stock items we need a program which will read through the table record by record and work out not only the value of that particular stock item but also the total value of the stock at the time. There is no need to give each item a stock number, its place in the list (its index) will be quite sufficient. So to work out the value of the stock we can write:

1. Initalize stockvalue to zero.
2. Loop while there are items to be read.
3.   Decode stockrecord into itemname, size, unitcost, number in stock, stock unit, date.
4.   Let item value:=unitcost/stockunit*number in stock.
5.   Let stockvalue:=stockvalue+item value.
6.   Print itemname, size, number in stock, item value.
7. Repeat.
8. Print stockvalue.

In our pseudo-code this becomes:

```
1. ARRAY stock$ (1:200)
2. LET value:=0
3. LET index:=1
4. LOOP WHILE there are records to be read
5.    EXECUTE READOUT(stock$(index),name$,size$,cost,number,
                      unit,date$)
6.    LET item:= cost/unit*number
7.    LET value:=value+item
8.    PRINT name$,number,size$,item
      LET index:=index+1
9. REPEAT
10.PRINT "Total value of stock:",value
```

**READOUT** is a program which is almost exactly the same as one already given and will read the values of the variables held in each record.

Having arrived at a very simple stock taking program we can now go on to a program to amend an entry in the **stock$** table.

112

However, before doing that it would probably be a good idea to have a regular listing of all the stock items in order to have a 'hard copy' of all the data held in the file. All that has to be done is to read every item and print the data in the following way:

1. Input date.
2. Print headings.
3. Loop while there are stock items to be read.
4.    Decode each record.
5.    Convert the date into day, month, year.
6.    Print itemname, size, unitcost, numberinstock, stockunit, day, month, year.
7. Repeat.

This then becomes:

```
1. ARRAY stock$ (1:200)
2. READ date$
3. PRINT "Stock position on ",date$
4. PRINT "STOCK ITEM","SALES UNIT","UNIT COST",
        "NO. IN STOCK","BUYING UNIT","LAST DELIVERY"
5. LET count:=1
6. LOOP WHILE there are records to be read
7.    EXECUTE READOUT(stock$(count),name$,size$,cost,number,
                      unit,date$)
8.    LET year$:= LEFT(date$,2)
9.    LET dayno:= RIGHT(date$,3)
10.   EXECUTE DAYIN(dayno,date$)
11.   PRINT count,name$,size$,cost,number,unit,date$,year$
12.   LET count:=count+1
13.REPEAT
```

Now we have a 'hard copy' of the data relating to every stock item. Our next task is to change any records which need amending as stock is sold and new deliveries are made. To do this we would:

1. Input date.
2. Input itemno.
3. Loop.
4.    Decode the data from the appropriate record.
5.    Print itemname, size.
6.    Input numberleft.
7.    Let numberinstock=numberleft.
8.    Input numberofcases,casecost.
9.    Let numberinstock=numberinstock+ numberofcases*stockunit.
10.   Assemble a new record.
11.   Replace the old record with the new record.
12.   Input itemno.
13.Repeat until itemno=0.

A pseudo-code program would be:

```
1.  ARRAY stock$ (1:200)
2.  PRINT "Date :DD/MM/YY"
3.  READ date$
4.  LET year$:=RIGHT(date$,2)
5.  LET date$:=LEFT(date$,5)
6.  EXECUTE DAYOUT(date$,dayno)
7.  PRINT "Item number:"
8.  READ index
9.  LOOP
10.    EXECUTE READOUT(stock$(index),name$,size$,cost,number,
                       unit,date$)
11.    PRINT name$,size$
12.    PRINT "How many in stock ?"
13.    READ left
14.    LET number:=left
15.    PRINT "How many cases delivered ?"
16.    READ cases
17.    PRINT "Has the cost per case changed ?"
18.    READ reply$
19.    IF reply$="YES"
20.       THEN
21.          PRINT "New cost per case:"
22.          READ cost
23.       ELSE
24.          SKIP
25.    IFEND
26.    LET number:=number+cases*unit
27.    LET date$:=year$+dayno$
28.    EXECUTE WRITEIN(stock$(index),name$,size$,cost,number,
                       unit,date$)
29.    PRINT "Item number"
30.    READ index
31. REPEAT UNTIL index=0
```

Note that the instructions on lines 13 and 14 will take account of a reduction in stock, especially if there is no delivery—i.e., **cases** is set to zero in line 16. The subprogram WRITEIN will reassemble the record and write it back to **stock$(index)**. That is another short program which you are being left to write yourselves.

These programs can just as easily be used to keep track of the stock of a sweetshop or any retail outlet where the range of stock stays fairly constant but is moving in a regular manner.

# Project 7—Text analysis

The analysis of text can prove a very fascinating and rewarding project. There are so many things one can do in this field and it is hoped that the suggestions made here will start you off on a number of interesting paths. First of all, however, there need to be a number of tools placed at your disposal. The first of these will be a subprogram which will enable you to separate a piece of text into its individual words. This subprogram is designed to be presented with a string of characters called **text$** and returns

**114**

the first complete word in that string. The string of characters held in **text$** is then set to be the remainder of the original string after the word has been removed. In other words if we write

EXECUTE WORD(**text$,word$**)

where **text$** is 'All things bright and beautiful' then **word$** becomes 'All' and **text$** becomes 'things bright and beautiful'.

1. Read text$.
2. Place a blank in word$.
3. Loop.
4.   Add next character in text$ onto word$.
5. Repeat until a space or a full-stop is reached.
6. Replace text$ with rest of text following the space or the full-stop.

But wait! English text normally contains other characters apart from letters of the alphabet and full-stops. How do we deal with commas, exclamation marks, semi-colons, and so forth? We will have to tell our program to ignore such characters. So we must modify line 4 by writing:

4.   Add the next character in text$ onto word$ unless the character is ; or : or ? or # or ,.

```
SUBPROGRAM WORD(text$,word$)
1. LET index:=1
2. LET word$:=""
3. LOOP
4.   IF text$(index)=";" OR text$(index)=":" OR
        text$(index)="?" OR text$(index)="!" OR
        text$(index)=","
5.     THEN
6.       LET index:=index+1
7.     ELSE
8.       LET word$:=word$+text$(index)
9.       LET index:=index+1
10.    IFEND
11.REPEAT UNTIL text$(index)=" " OR text$(index)="."
12.LET text$:=RIGHT(text$,length-index)
13.RETURN TO MAIN PROGRAM
```

This subprogram can now be used to count the number of words in a piece of text, since we can write:

1. Read text$.
2. Let numberofwords=0.
3. Loop while text$<>"".
4.   Execute WORD(text$,word$).

5. Let numberofwords=numberofwords+1.
6. Repeat.
7. Print numberofwords.

In pseudo-code this becomes:

```
1. READ text$
2. LET words:=0
3. LOOP WHILE text$<>""
4.    EXECUTE WORD(text$,word$)
5.    LET words:=words+1
6. REPEAT
7. PRINT words
```

We can easily count the number of letters in each word by storing the length of each word—LEN in BASIC. So now we should be able to read a sentence, count the number of words in it, and calculate the average length of each word in the sentence. This often provides a good clue to the authorship of a piece of writing. Before we do this, however, we should make sure that our program will be able to identify the end of a sentence. So we should amend WORD slightly to take account of that:

```
SUBPROGRAM WORD(text$,word$,flag)
1. LET flag:=0
2. LET index:=1
3. LET word$:=""
4. LOOP
5.    IF text$(index)=";" OR text$(index)=":" OR
         text$(index)="?" OR text$(index)="!" OR
         text$(index)=","
6.       THEN
7.          LET index:=index+1
8.       ELSE
9.          LET word$:=word$+text$(index)
10.         LET index:=index+1
11.      IFEND
12.REPEAT UNTIL text$(index)=" " OR text$(index)="."
13.IF text$(index)="."
14.    THEN
15.       LET flag:=1
16.    ELSE
17.       SKIP
18.IFEND
19.LET text$:=RIGHT(text$,length-index)
END OF SUBPROGRAM
```

The value of **flag** tells us whether or not the full-stop which signifies the end of the sentence has been reached.

Now we are in a position to read a piece of text, count the number of words in each sentence, and calculate the average number of words per sentence and the average number of letters per word:

1. Read text$.
2. Let numberofsentences=0.
3. Let numberofwords=0.

**116**

4. Let numberofletters=0.
5. Loop while text$<>".
6.    Execute WORD(text$,word$,flag).
7.    Let numberofletters=numberofletters+lengthword.
8.    Let numberofwords=numberofwords+1.
9.    If flag=1
10.     Then let numberofsentences=numberofsentences+1.
11.     Else do nothing.
12.    Ifend.
13. Repeat.
14. Let avword=numberofletters/numberofwords.
15. Let avsent= numberofwords/numberofsentences.
16. Print numberofsentences,numberofwords,
numberofletters,avword,avsent.

In pseudo-code we can write:

```
1. READ text$
2. LET sentence:=0
3. LET words:=0
4. LET letters:=0
5. LOOP WHILE text$<>""
6.    EXECUTE WORD(text$,word$,flag)
7.    LET letters:=letters+lengthword
8.    LET words:=words+1
9.    IF flag=1
10.       THEN
11.          LET sentence:=sentence+1
12.       ELSE
13.          SKIP
14.    IFEND
15. REPEAT
16. LET avword:=letters/words
17. LET avsent:=words/sentence
18. PRINT "Total number of letters in the text:",
          letters
19. PRINT "Total number of words in the text:",words
20. PRINT "Average number of letters per word:",avword
21. PRINT "Average number of words per sentence:",
          avsent
```

This program works very satisfactorily but note what happens if you follow a full-stop by a space before the first character of the next sentence. Remember also that the maximum length of text which can usually be stored in **text$** is 255 characters, so you may have to break up a long piece of text into pieces no more than that length and read them from a list, thus **text$** becomes **text$ (index)**, as we have used many times before.

Finally, in this project we can use our WORD subprogram to search for the number of times a particular word occurs in a piece of text; word frequency is another 'detective' technique which can be used to establish the authorship of a work. All we need to do is to say:

1. Read text$.
2. Read search$.
3. Let count=0.
4. Loop while text$<>".
5.     Execute WORD(text$,word$,flag).
6.     If search$=word$ then let count=count+1.
7. Repeat.
8. If count=0 then print search$, "not found".
9. Else print search$, "occurred", count, "times".

which becomes:

```
1. READ text$
2. PRINT "Word to be searched for:"
3. READ search$
4. LET count:=0
5. LOOP WHILE text$<>""
6.     EXECUTE WORD(text$,word$,flag)
7.     IF search$=word$
8.     THEN
9.         LET count:=count+1
10.    ELSE
11.        SKIP
12.    IFEND
13.REPEAT    .
14.IF count=0
15.    THEN
16.        PRINT search$,"not found"
17.    ELSE
18.        PRINT search$,"occurred",count,"times"
19.IFEND
```

This is quite a simple program to write but beware of one large pitfall. It is that words can occur either within a sentence or at the beginning of a sentence. This means that although we know that 'Hotel' and 'hotel' are the same word the computer does not. Remember the indexing problem, Project 1. Thus you will have to either make the search for both versions of the word by having **search1$**='Hotel' and **search2$**='hotel' and making line 7 read:

```
7. IF search1$=word$ or search2$=word$
```

or by actually looking at the codes used by the computer to store the characters. These are called ASCII (American Standard Code for Information Interchange) codes. If you do this you will discover that the letter 'H' is stored as the number 72 and the letter 'h' is stored as the number 104 (72 + 32). In fact you will find that the ASCII code for any lower case letter is 32 + the ASCII code for the same letter in upper case. If you use this fact you can make use of the BASIC functions ASC and CHR$ to get

118

your program to make two words to be searched for out of the one you input. An interesting little exercise!

## Project 8—Text editing

Text editing is the manipulation of strings of characters held in the computer's memory. When taken to very sophisticated levels text editing becomes 'word processing' and it was, in fact, with a word processing program that the text for this book was created. It saved the author having to retype pages of text whenever an alteration, large or small, was made. The insertion and deletion of letters, or even whole paragraphs, is made very easy by the use of text editing programs. Not only that,but the 'justification' of type so that there is no ragged right-hand edge to the text can now be left for the computer to do.In addition it proves to be a very simple task to effect changes to the text, e.g., changing every occurrence of the word 'my' to 'our'.

Let us look at how some of these operations can be performed. The first one to deal with is REPLACE where we will write a subprogram which will replace one set of characters by another. We will call the set of characters to be replaced **pattern$** and the set of characters which will take their place will be called **replacement$**. Our top-down approach starts off as:

1. Read text$.
2. Read pattern$.
3. Read replacement$.
4. Find the first occurrence of pattern$ in text$.
5. Replace pattern$ by replacement$ in text$.

But how do we discover at what point in text$ our pattern$ will match? We can do this by testing pattern$ against text$ in the following way. Suppose we want to replace the letters 'my' by 'our' in the sentence

'We returned to my home last night'

If we test in sequence and count along the text string as follows:

'We returned to my home last night'
'my'                                                         first test,no match
'We returned to my home last night'
 'my'                                                        second test,no match
'We returned to my home last night'
  'my'                                                       third test,no match

'We returned to my home last night'
 'my'                                    fourth test, no match

we eventually get:

'We returned to my home last night'
                'my'                     sixteenth test, MATCH

at which point we can split text$ into two parts, one to the left of the matching point and one to the right. We can then expand line 4 to read:

4a. Count the number of characters we have to advance along text$ until we find a match.
4b. Split text$ into a left-hand part at the point where the match occurred.
4c. Take the right-hand part of text$ from the end of the matching sequence to the end of text$.

Then line 5 can be rewritten as:

5. Create a new version of text$ by setting up the string formed by the left-hand part, the replacement, and the right-hand part.

In pseudo-code this can be written as:

```
SUBPROGRAM REPLACE(text$,pattern$,replacement$)
1. LOOP FOR index = 1 TO lengthtext
2.    IF pattern$=text$(index,lengthpattern-1)
3.      THEN
4.         LET left$:=LEFT(text$,index-1)
5.         LET right$:=RIGHT(text$,lengthtext-
                                  (index+lengthpattern-1))
6.         LET text$:=left$+replacement$+right$
7.         RETURN TO MAIN PROGRAM
8.      ELSE
9.         SKIP
10.   IFEND
11.REPEAT
END OF SUBPROGRAM
```

The next step is to write a subprogram called REPLACEALL which will allow us to replace every occurrence of **pattern$** with **replacement$** in the string called **text$**. First of all let us write:

1. Read text$.
2. Read pattern$.

**120**

3. Read replacement$.
4. Let newtext$="""
5. Loop for index=1 to lengthtext.
6.    Set test$=text$(index,lengthpattern-1).
7.    If test$=pattern$ then set newtext$=newtext$+ replacement$ and set index=index+lengthpattern-1.
8.    Else set newtext$=newtext$+text$(index).
9. Repeat.
10.Set text$=newtext$.

In pseudo-code this can be written as:

```
SUBPROGRAM REPLACEALL(text$,pattern$,replacement$)
1. LET newtext$:=""
2. LOOP FOR index=1 TO length
3.    LET test$:=text$(index,lengthpattern-1)
4.    IF test$=pattern$
5.       THEN
6.          LET newtext$:=newtext$+replacement$
7.          LET index:=index+lengthpattern-1
8.       ELSE
9.          LET newtext$:=newtext$+text$(index)
10.   IFEND
11.REPEAT
12.LET text$:=newtext$
END OF SUBPROGRAM
```

As a reminder, in the pseudo-code **text$** (**a,b**) means the part of the string called **text$** from the **a**th character to the **b**th character. and **text$** (**k**) means the **k**th character in the string called **text$**.

One point to notice about both of the above programs is that there is no provision, and there ought to be, for telling the user that the characters to be replaced have not been found. But that is something for the reader to put in himself.

In order to insert a new character or string of characters into an existing string we can write a routine called INSERT, but first we need a subprogram which will split a string into two parts at some predetermined point:

1. Read text$.
2. Read pointer.
3. Set left$=LEFT(text$,pointer).
4. Set right$=RIGHT(text$,lengthtext-pointer).

In other words:

```
SUBPROGRAM SPLIT(text$,left$,right$,pointer)
1. LET left$:=LEFT(text$,pointer)
2. LET right$:=RIGHT(text$,length-pointer)
END OF SUBPROGRAM
```

In order to insert a piece of text we can write:

1. Read text$.
2. Read extra$.
3. Read pointer.
4. Execute SPLIT(text$,left$,right$,pointer).
5. Set text$=left$+extra$+right$.

We then get:

```
1. PRINT "At what character do you want the extra inserting ?"
2. READ pointer
3. PRINT "Extra character(s) ?"
4. READ extra$
5. EXECUTE SPLIT(text$,left$,right$,pointer)
6. LET text$:=left$+extra$+right$
```

Perhaps for completeness we should have a FIND subprogram which will search through a piece of text to see if a particular set of characters exists in the text. It is quite possible that the whole of the text is too large to fit onto the screen and so it should be possible to dispatch the computer to find the characters specified and report back on the whereabouts of those characters. We have already done something of this nature in the REPLACE subprogram, so all we need to do is modify that:

1. Read text$.
2. Read pattern$.
3. Find the first occurrence of pattern$ in text$.
4. Record the position of the first occurrence of pattern$.

Then we can write:

```
SUBPROGRAM FIND(text$,pattern$,pointer)
1. LET pointer:=0
2. LOOP FOR index = 1 TO lengthtext
3.    IF pattern$=text$(index,lengthpattern-1)
4.       THEN
5.          LET pointer:=index
6.          RETURN TO MAIN PROGRAM
7.       SKIP
8.    IFEND
9. REPEAT
END OF SUBPROGRAM
```

Finally we want to be able to write a program which will output text with any length of line and with a straight right-hand margin. For example, the text:

'What we have to do is to break up the text string into pieces which are of the required line length. However there is a problem here because we do not want to split words up just to create the correct line length. So we have to make sure that each line contains whole words and then we insert spaces between the words in order to make the lines all of the same length.'

can be printed like this:

What we have to do is to break up the text string into pieces which are of the required length. However there is a problem here because we do not want to split words up just to create the correct line length. So we have to make sure that each line contains whole words in order to make the lines all of the same length.

or like this:

> What we have to do is to break up the text string into pieces which are of the required line length. However there is a problem here because we do not want to split words up just to create the correct line length. So we have to make sure that each line contains whole words and then we insert spaces between the words in order to make the lines all of the same length.

What we have to do is this:

1.  Read text$.
2.  Copy text$ into string$.
3.  Read linelength.
4.  Loop.
5.     Set newtext$ to ".
6.     Loop while length of newtext$<=linelength.
7.        Execute WORD1(string$,word$).
8.        If length of newtext$+length of word$<=linelength
9.          Then set newtext$=newtext$+word$.
10.         Else replace word$ in string$.
11.       Ifend.
12.     Repeat.
13.    Execute JUSTIFY(newtext$,linelength).
14.    Print newtext$.
15. Repeat until string$=" or lengthstring<=linelength
16. If lengthstring<=linelength.

17. Then print string$.
18. Else do nothing.
19.Ifend.

The reason for the last few lines of the program is to take account of the fact that sooner or later we are going to be left with a string in string$ which will fit comfortably into a line without any additional padding. If this is the case the string can be printed unjustified.

The reason for copying the original text into another string is to ensure that the original text is left untouched and only the copy is gradually reduced to an empty string. Notice how we can write our program in such a way that we can look at the overall strategy without having to worry about the details of the actual JUSTIFY program. That will come later.

The subprogram WORD1 will be very similar to the WORD subprogram in the previous project but without the tests, where the punctuation marks are ignored. These either have to be treated as part of the word which precedes them or as words in their own right. This is another small task left to the reader to experiment with.

Our pseudo-code program becomes:

```
1.  READ text$
2.  LET string$:=text$
3.  PRINT "What line length is required ?"
4.  READ linelength
5.  LOOP
6.     LET newtext$:=""
7.        LOOP WHILE lengthnewtext<=linelength
8.           EXECUTE WORD1(string$,word$)
9.           IF lengthnewtext+lengthword<=linelength
10.             THEN
11.                LET newtext$:=newtext$+word$
12.             ELSE
13.                LET string$:=string$+word$
14.          IFEND
15.       REPEAT
16.    EXECUTE JUSTIFY(newtext$,linelength)
17.    PRINT newtext$
18. REPEAT UNTIL string$="" OR lengthstring<=linelength
19. IF lengthstring<=linelength
20.    THEN
21.       PRINT string$
22.    ELSE
23.       SKIP
24. IFEND
```

Now we can concentrate on JUSTIFY which has a piece of text with spaces between the words and a target line length into which the text must fit exactly. If the length of the text is equal to the line length then there is no problem, but if it is less then extra spaces have to be inserted until the length of the text string is exactly right. Now the number of spaces in the string is equal to one less than the number of words in the string, and the difference between the line length and the actual length of the string is the number of extra spaces which have to be inserted. What has to be done in JUSTIFY is therefore to allocate these extra spaces according to some rule. There are obviously going to be a number of ways this can be done, but for the purpose of this example we shall say that we will add the extra spaces in turn to the spaces which already exist. In other words, if the line contains seven words and there are an extra three spaces needed to make it the correct length, then the first three spaces of the seven will have an extra space added. If, however, an extra nine spaces are needed then the first three spaces have two extra spaces added and the remaining three have one space added. Hence we can write:

1. Read text$.
2. Read linelength.
3. Set spaces = 0.
4. Set extra = linelength - lengthtext.
5. Scan through text$ and add 1 to spaces each time a space is found.
6. Set number of additional spaces to the whole number obtained by dividing extra by spaces.
7. Set up newtext$ by adding extra spaces to all the spaces in text$.
8. Set remaining spaces to be added by subtracting the production of extra and spaces from the number of additional spaces needed.
9. If number of additional spaces = 0 then print the newtext$ and stop.
10. Else print newtext$ character by character adding an extra space to the first extra spaces.

A pseudo-code program would be:

```
SUBPROGRAM JUSTIFY(text$,linelength)
1.  LET spaces:=0
2.  LET extra:=linelength-lengthtext
3.  LOOP FOR index=1 TO lengthtext
4.     IF text$(index)=" "
5.        THEN
6.           LET spaces:=spaces+1
7.        ELSE
8.           SKIP
9.     IFEND
10.REPEAT
11.LET number:=CHOP(extra/spaces)
12.LET newtext$:=" "
13.LOOP FOR index=1 TO lengthtext
14.    LET newtext$:=newtext$+text$(index)
```

```
15.    IF text$=" "
16.     THEN
17.        LOOP FOR count=1 TO number
18.          LET newtext$:=newtext$+" "
19.        REPEAT
20.     ELSE
21.        SKIP
22.    IFEND
23.REPEAT
24.LET remain:=extra-spaces*number
25.IF remain=0
26.  THEN
27.     PRINT newtext$
28.     STOP
29.  ELSE
30.     LET index=0
31.     LOOP FOR count=1 to remain
32.        LET index:=index+1
33.        LOOP WHILE newtext$<>" "
34.           PRINT newtext$(index)
35.           LET index:=index+1
36.        REPEAT
37.        PRINT newtext$(index)
38.        LOOP WHILE newtext$(index)=" "
39.           PRINT " "
40.           LET index:=index+1
41.        REPEAT
42.        PRINT newtext$(index)
43.     REPEAT
44.IFEND
45.PRINT RIGHT(newtext$,lengthnewtext-index)
END OF SUBPROGRAM
```

# Project 9—A school timetable

This is not a project to do all the school timetabling for you.
What it does, however, is to set up a master timetable and make
it possible for a large number of details about it to be easily
extracted. In the 'pencil and paper' method we have one sheet
per day and this is divided up into squares, usually with times
starting at 9.00 a.m. from left to right across the top and with
the room numbers set out downwards from top left to bottom
left. In each square we write the class identification and the
teacher's name:

| | 9.15 – 9.45 | 9.45 – 10.15 | 10.30 – 11.00 | 11.00–30 |
|---|---|---|---|---|
| 1 | 1(a) E.Green Ma. | 1(a) E.Green Ma. | 3(c) F.Butt Sc. | 1(a) G.Hunt Ar. |
| 2 | 2(b) F.Butt Sc. | 4(g) A.Wass Hi. | 3(d) F.Brown En. | 3(c) J.Jones Ge. |
| 3 | 3(a) K.Walsh Ge. | 4(a) T.Toms Ma. | 5(c) E.Green Ma. | 5(a) T.Toms Ma. |
| 4 | 2(a) G.Hunt Ar. | 4(b) W.Patel Sc. | 1(a) W.Patel Sc. | 2(a) R.Short SS |

126

Each entry in the table records the class number, the name of the teacher and a subjects code, where Ma. stands for Mathematics, Sc. for Science, and so on.

From this table we can find which rooms are occupied by which teacher, which rooms are occupied by which class, the timetable for each teacher, the timetable for each class, and so on. At first sight it would seem that just one table for each day would be appropriate with all the information we need on that table. However, it is probably better to have three tables for each day: one table for the classes, another for the teachers, and another for the subjects. We thus obtain a table, let us call it **class$**, which looks like this:

|   | 1 | 2 | 3 | 4 |
|---|---|---|---|---|
| 1 | 1(a) | 1(a) | 3(c) | 1(a) |
| 2 | 2(b) | 4(g) | 3(d) | 3(c) |
| 3 | 3(a) | 4(a) | 5(c) | 5(a) |
| 4 | 2(a) | 4(b) | 1(a) | 2(a) |

The table called **teachers$** would look like this:

|   | 1 | 2 | 3 | 4 |
|---|---|---|---|---|
| 1 | E.Green | E.Green | F.Butt | G.Hunt |
| 2 | F.Butt | A.Wass | F.Brown | J.Jones |
| 3 | K.Walsh | T.Toms | E.Green | T.Toms |
| 4 | G.Hunt | W.Patel | W.Patel | R.Short |

and the table called **subjects$** would be:

|   | 1 | 2 | 3 | 4 |
|---|---|---|---|---|
| 1 | Ma. | Ma. | Sc. | Ar. |
| 2 | Sc. | Hi. | En. | Ge. |
| 3 | Ge. | Ma. | Ma. | Ma. |
| 4 | Ar. | Sc. | Sc. | SS |

The contents of each table will be identified by two numbers. The column number is the period number of the day and the row number identifies the room. What we have created here is called a 'data structure' and defines exactly the way in which our information is stored. We have used data structures in this book already, but not such complex ones. Each day of the working week will have its own **class$**, **teachers$**, and **subject$** table. Our problem will devote itself to just looking at the timetable for one day only. The concept can easily be extended to cover all the working days.

Our task will as usual be in several parts. One of these will be to search the table to see what rooms are empty at specific times and to list these. Initially all the entries in each table will be empty and the tables will fill up with data as rooms are allocated. So what we have to do is to search one of the tables looking for blanks. Because we are searching tables and not lists we have to decide how we are to do it. Let us look through the table **class$** and search for blanks. We will do it row by row (i.e., room by room) and throughout the day period by period (i.e., column by column):

1. Read table class$.
2. Set any$="no".
3. Loop for room = 1 to 25.
4.    Loop for period = 1 to 7.
5.       If class$(room,period)="".
6.         Then print room,period.
7.         Set any$="yes".
8.         Else do nothing.
9.       Ifend.
10.   Repeat.
11. Repeat.
12. If any$="no" then print "All rooms full".

This assumes that there are 25 rooms to choose from and 7 periods in the day. Notice the loop within a loop so that we find and print all the periods in a day when a particular room is vacant in room order. The variable **any$** enables a message to be printed which tells us if no vacant rooms are found.

The program in pseudo-code becomes:

```
PROGRAM FREE
1.  ARRAY class$
2.  LET any$:="no"
3.  LOOP FOR room=1 TO 25
4.     LOOP FOR period=1 to 7
5.        IF class$(room,period)=""
6.           THEN
7.              PRINT "Room",room,"Free in Period",period
8.              LET any$:="yes"
9.           ELSE
10.             SKIP
11.      IFEND
12.    REPEAT
13. REPEAT
14. IF any$="no"
15.    THEN
16.       PRINT "All rooms full"
17.    ELSE
18.       SKIP
RETURN TO MAIN MENU
```

**128**

If we want to place a 'booking' for a room we have to find if the room is free and if the member of staff is free at that time; and if so then the appropriate data can be entered in the tables.

First of all we need to specify the room number and the period number to see if the room is free, then we can specify the teacher to be assigned to the class and see if he/she is free at that time. We can do this by looking through the **teachers$** table for the period specified and seeing if the named teacher is allocated to another class at that time — teachers cannot be in two places at once! If both these tests are successful then all three tables can be amended.

1. Read room.
2. Read period.
3. Read teachersname$.
4. Read table class$.
5. Read table teachers$.
6. Read table subject$.
7. If class$(room,period)=""
8.     Then loop for roomno = 1 to 25.
9.         If teachers$(roomno,period)=teachersname$
10.           Then print teachername$,"not available".
11.              Stop.
12.           Else do nothing.
13.       Ifend.
14.       Repeat.
15.       Read classname$.
16.       Read subjectcode$.
17.       Set teachers$(room,period)=teachersname$.
18.       Set class$(room,period)=classname$.
19.       Set subject$(room,period)=subjectcode$.
20.    Else print "Room not available".
21.Ifend.

We can write this as:

```
PROGRAM ALLOCATE
1.  ARRAY class$(1:25,1:7)
2.  ARRAY teachers$(1:25,1:7)
3.  ARRAY subject$(1:25,1:5)
4.  PRINT "Room number required"
5.  READ room
6.  PRINT "For period"
7.  READ period
8.  PRINT "Teacher"
9.  READ name$
10. IF class$(room,period)=""
11.    THEN
12.      LOOP FOR roomno=1 TO 25
```

**129**

```
13.        IF teachers$(roomno,period)=name$
14.          THEN
15.            PRINT name$,"not available"
17.            RETURN TO MAIN MENU
18.          ELSE
19.            SKIP
20.        IFEND
21.      REPEAT
22.      PRINT "Class name"
23.      READ cname$
24.      PRINT "Subject code"
25.      READ code$
26.      LET teachers$(room,period):=name$
27.      LET class$(room,period):=cname$
28.      LET subject$(room,period):=code$
29.    ELSE
30.      PRINT "Room not available"
31.IFEND
RETURN TO MAIN MENU
```

Having distributed the data among the three tables we can extract these data in order to obtain the timetable for a class or a specific teacher. We are not going to write two programs for this; one is quite sufficient. What we have to do is to specify a table name and the type of information we wish to extract. In other words we write:

1. Print "Do you want a teacher or a class timetable ?".
2. Read reply$.
3. If reply$="teacher".
4.    Then read teachersname$,
        Print rooms,periods and classes taken by that teacher.
5.    Else read class number,
        Print rooms,periods,teachers and subjects for that class.
6. Ifend.

Again, this becomes:

```
PROGRAM PRINT
1. ARRAY class$(1:25,1:7)
2. ARRAY teachers$(1:25,1:7)
3. ARRAY subject$(1:25,1:7)
4. PRINT "Do you want a teacher or a class timetable?"
5. READ reply$
6. IF reply$="teacher"
7.    THEN
8.      READ name$
9.      LOOP FOR room=1 TO 25
10.        LOOP FOR period=1 TO 7
11.          IF teachers$(room,period)=name$
12.            THEN
13.              PRINT room,period,class$(room,period),
                      subject$(room,period)
14.            ELSE
15.              SKIP
16.            IFEND
17.        REPEAT
18.      REPEAT
19.    ELSE
20.      READ classname$
```

**130**

```
21.     LOOP FOR room=1 TO 25
22.       LOOP FOR period=1 TO 7
23.         IF class$(room,period)=classname$
24.           THEN
25.             PRINT room,period,teachers$(room,period),
                  subject$(room,period)
26.           ELSE
27.             SKIP
28.         IFEND
29.       REPEAT
30.     REPEAT
31. IFEND
RETURN TO MAIN MENU
```

The structure of the menu will be:

1. SELECT **number** FROM 4 CASES
2. CASE 1
3.    CHAIN PRINT
4. CASE 2
5.    CHAIN ALLOCATE
6. CASE 3
7.    CHAIN FREE
8. CASE 4
9.    STOP
10. DEFAULT
11.    PRINT "Only the numbers 1,2,3, or 4 are acceptable"
12. SELECTEND

This approach to data which are normally held in a table where each entry holds several different pieces of information can be applied to, say, a hotel booking system where the problems are very similar. What has been done of course is to produce a series of tables as one would produce a series of transparencies, one overlaying another, but each layer of transparency only holds one type of information. Each 'layer' can be searched separately without elaborate decoding routines and this must in the long run produce programs which are easier to write, understand, and modify.

**Project 10—Data validation**
In all the programs written so far there is very little included about the very important topic of data validation. If data are to be processed by your computer then it is best to make sure that the data are good data and not rubbish. Incorrect data are often entered by accident when a wrong key is pressed by someone unfamiliar with using a keyboard. It is also very easy for numbers to be transcribed from paper to keyboard incorrectly. For example, the number 45679 can be transcribed as 45769 or

35568 as 35668. Whenever possible these errors should be detected and corrected—if not by the operator then by the program. There is a well-known phrase in computing circles— GIGO, meaning 'Garbage In is Garbage Out'. We do not want our elegantly constructed program to be sent off into an infinite loop simply because someone has given it wrong information. Errors really fall into two types. The first of these is the incorrect entering of data, for the reasons already mentioned. The second type of error is what is known as a 'reconciliation' error. This type of error is where perfectly acceptable data are processed incorrectly by the program because allowances have not been made for certain situations. We have in fact met this type of error where we are, for example, searching for a name in a list and the name does not exist anywhere in the list. A program, such as SEARCH in Project 3, which has to find a name on a mailing list should return a message saying what has happened if **name$** is not on the list being searched. If this is not done the variable **record$** which the subprogram returns will cause DECODE to process the wrong record.

What this project will do is to provide some subprograms which will check for obvious mistakes in data entry by suitable checking routines. The only way to trap reconciliation errors is to write programs in such a way that such errors are detected as they occur and before they can wreck your processing.

A common type of error which can be detected by a simple routine is that caused by the input of an obviously wrong date. For example, the date 30 February 1983 is incorrect, as is 31 September 1983 or 30 June 1893—at least if it is intended to be a date in the current year!

First of all we will devise a routine which will check a date which is input in the form of:

DD/MM/YY

which is a string such that the first two characters are the day of the month, characters 4 and 5 are the month of the year, and the last two characters are the year. Our DATECHECK subprogram will be able to detect an invalid date of the form

31/02/83

or

01/03/93

132

when the current year is 1983.

Our strategy will therefore be to reconcile the day of the month with the month of the year and discover whether the day number can in fact lie in that month. The first thing therefore will be to set up a list which contains the number of days in each month of the current year. Then we shall test to see if the day number is less than or equal to the number of days in the specified month. Then we will check the year for being reasonable in the context of the data being input.

1. Set up a list containing the number of days in each of the 12 months of the year.
2. Read date$ in the form DD/MM/YY.
3. Set currentyear=83.
4. Set dayno=LEFT(date$,2).
5. Set monthno=date$(4,2).
6. Set yearno=RIGHT(date$,2)
7. Set valid$='yes'.
8. If monthno>12
9.    Then set valid$="no".
10.       Stop.
11.    Else if dayno>list(monthno).
12.       Then set valid$="no".
13.          Stop.
14.       Else if yearno>currentyear
15.          Then set valid$="no".
16.          Else do nothing
17.          Ifend.
18.       Ifend.
19.    Ifend.
20.If valid$="no".
21.    Then print "Year  s 19", yearno, "Is this OK?".
22.       Read reply$.
23.       If reply$="OK".
24.          Then set valid$="yes".
25.             Stop.
26.          Else.
27.             Do nothing.
28.       Ifend.
29.Ifend.

Writing this in pseudo-code we get:

```
SUPROGRAM DATECHECK(date$,valid$)
1. ARRAY list(1:12)
```

```
2. LOOP for index=1 to 12
3.    LET list(index):=31,28,31,30,31,30,31,31,30,31,30,31
4. REPEAT
5. LET currentyear:=83
6. LET dayno:=LEFT(date$,2)
7. LET monthno:=date$(4,2)
8. LET yearno:=RIGHT(date$,2)
9. LET valid$:="yes"
10.IF monthno>12
11.    THEN
12.       LET valid$:="no"
13.       RETURN TO MAIN PROGRAM
14.    ELSE
15.       IF dayno>list(monthno)
16.          THEN
17.             LET valid$:="no"
18.             RETURN TO MAIN PROGRAM
19.          ELSE
20.             IF yearno>currentyear
21.                THEN
22.                   LET valid$:="no"
23.                ELSE
24.                   SKIP
25.             IFEND
26.       IFEND
27.IFEND
28.IF valid$="no"
29.    THEN
30.       PRINT "Year is 19",yearno,"Is this OK?"
31.       READ reply$
32.       IF reply$="yes"
33.          THEN
34.             LET valid$:="yes"
35.          ELSE
36.             SKIP
37.       IFEND
38.IFEND
END OF SUBPROGRAM
```

A section of program which will use DATECHECK would look like this:

```
1. PRINT "Type in the date in the form DD/MM/YY"
2. READ date$
3. LET valid$="no"
4. LOOP WHILE valid$="no"
5.    EXECUTE DATECHECK(date$,valid$)
6.    IF valid$="no"
7.       THEN
8.          PRINT "Invalid date. Try again"
9.          READ date$
10.      ELSE
11.         SKIP
12.   IFEND
13.REPEAT
```

Now for another form of check. This is the type of check which can be made on, say, a part number and involves the use of a check digit. A good example is the ISBN (International Standard Book Number) which is allotted to every book in print. One such number might be 0 333 32018 2. Notice that the number consists of ten digits, the last of which is known as a check digit. The actual number used to identify the book is made up of the first nine digits and the last digit is specially

**134**

calculated to fulfil a specific rule. This rule is that the first digit is multiplied by 10, the second by 9, the third by 8, and so on up to the tenth digit. The numbers resulting from these calculations are then added together and their sum divided by 11. The result must be a whole number, i.e., no remainder. If this is the case then the ISBN is a valid number. If there is a remainder then the number input is not valid and must be rentered. As an example, for the ISBN which is 0 333 32018 2 we get:

$$
\begin{array}{rcl}
0 \times 10 & = & 0 \\
3 \times 9 & = & 27 \\
3 \times 8 & = & 24 \\
3 \times 7 & = & 21 \\
3 \times 6 & = & 18 \\
2 \times 5 & = & 10 \\
0 \times 4 & = & 0 \\
1 \times 3 & = & 3 \\
8 \times 2 & = & 16 \\
2 \times 1 & = & 2 \\
\end{array}
$$

Total            121

and 121 is an exact multiple of 11. Therefore we need two programs. One of these will check the final number for validity and the other will take the nine digits which form the actual ISBN and calculate the tenth digit which acts as a check digit. The second of these programs will multiply the first digit by 10, the second by 9, and so on until the ninth and last digit is multiplied by 2. Then the results of these multiplications are summed and divided by 11. The remainder is subtracted from 11 and this becomes the check digit which is placed at the end of the existing nine digits. You may at this point ask what happens if the remainder is 1. This would mean a check digit of 10, and we cannot have that. What is done in this case is to use the character "X" as the check digit. Let us sketch out our progrε n for calculating the check digit.

1. Read isbn$.
2. If lengthisbn<>9
3.     Then print "Only 9 digits required".
4.       Stop.
5.     Else set total=0.
6.       Set number=10.
7.       Loop for count=1 to 9.

8.        Set amount=isbn$(count).
9.        Set total=total+amount*number.
10.      Set number=number-1.
11.    Repeat.
12.    Set remain=MOD(total/11)
13.    If remain=10
14.      Then set remain$="X".
15.      Else do nothing.
16.    Ifend.
17.    Set isbn$=isbn$+remain$.
18.Ifend.

We can write this in pseudo-code as:

```
SUBPROGRAM SETISBN(isbn$)
1.  IF lengthisbn<>9
2.     THEN
3.        PRINT "9 digits required"
4.        RETURN TO MAIN PROGRAM
5.     ELSE
6.        LET total:=0
7.        LET number:=10
8.        LOOP FOR count=1 TO 9
9.           LET amount:=isbn$(count)
10.          LET total:=total+number*amount
11.          LET number:=number-1
12.       REPEAT
13.       LET remain:=11 - MOD(total,11)
14.       IF remain=10
15.          THEN
16.             LET remain$="X"
17.          ELSE
18.             SKIP
19.       IFEND
20.       LET isbn$:=isbn$+remain$
21.IFEND
END OF SUBPROGRAM
```

The subprogram to check the validity of an ISBN, CHECKISBN, would be very similar:

```
SUBPROGRAM CHECKISBN(isbn$,valid$)
1.  LET valid$:="no"
2.  IF lengthisbn<>10
3.     THEN
4.        RETURN TO MAIN PROGRAM
5.     ELSE
6.        LET total:=0
7.        LET number:=10
8.        LOOP FOR count=1 to 9
9.           LET amount:=isbn$(count)
10.          LET total:=total+number*amount
11.          LET number:=number-1
12.       REPEAT
13.       IF isbn$(10)="X"
14.          THEN
15.             LET amount=10
16.          ELSE
17.             LET amount:=isbn$(10)
```

```
18.      IFEND
19.      LET total:=total+number*amount
20.      IF total/11=CHOP(total/11)
21.         THEN
22.            LET valid$:="yes"
23.         ELSE
24.            SKIP
25       IFEND
26. IFEND
END OF SUBPROGRAM
```

There are other kinds of error which cannot be trapped by the above kind of test. An error of transposition when we are entering, say, a book number can be picked up by having a check digit, but an error of transposition in entering, for example, an amount of money or a reading from an electricity meter cannot be detected by this type of test. All that can be tested for is whether the number falls within certain limits. Suppose an amount of money was entered without the decimal point separating pounds from pence—45632 instead of 456.32. This could at least be signalled by the program insisting that a whole number of pounds is entered as, say, 45632.00. The program would look for a decimal point in the third position from the right and if one were not found it should ask for the amount to be reentered in the correct form:

1. Read amount$.
2. Check to see if the third character from the end is a "." character.
3. If the character is "." then proceed.
4. If not, ask for a reentry.

We can write this in pseudo-code as:

```
SUBPROGRAM CHECKAMOUNT(amount$)
1. LOOP WHILE amount$(lengthamount-2)<>"."
2.    PRINT "Please enter the amount in form XXXXX.XX"
3.    READ amount$
4. REPEAT
RETURN TO MAIN PROGRAM
```

In a similar manner we can check to see if a name consists only of valid characters. For example if the name "HENRY" were accidentally entered as "HEN3RY" then there is little point in allowing the program to start, say, searching for the name—let alone actually letting it search. The search will be a complete waste of time and will never be successful. So what we need to do is to trap out the obvious errors on the entry of words in order to see that only a certain set of characters exist in each entry. What we can do is to:

**137**

1. Read word$.
2. Check each character in word$ against a list of acceptable characters.
3. If any character not in the list is found in word$.
4. Then ask for word$ to be input again.

Again we can write:

```
SUBPROGRAM CHECKWORD(word$,valid$)
1. LET valid$:="yes"
2. LET testchars$:="ABCDEFGHIJKLMNOPQRSTUVWXYZ"
3. LOOP FOR index=1 TO lengthword
4.     LET count:=1
5.     LOOP WHILE word$(index)<>testchars$(count)
6.        LET count:=count+1
7.        IF count=27
8.           THEN
9.              LET valid$:="no"
10.             RETURN TO MAIN PROGRAM
11.          ELSE
12.             SKIP
13.       IFEND
14.    REPEAT
15.REPEAT
RETURN TO MAIN PROGRAM
```

## To use the subprogram we could write:

```
1. LET ok$:="no"
2. LOOP WHILE ok$="no"
3.    READ word$
4.    EXECUTE CHECKWORD(word$,ok$)
5.    IF ok$="no"
6.       THEN
7.          PRINT "Non-alphabetic character(s) in",word$
8.       ELSE
9.          SKIP
10.   IFEND
11.REPEAT
```

# 6 INDEX OF SUBPROGRAMS AND ROUTINES